DRAW-BRIDGES

DRAW-BRIDGES

Activities and Ideas for Incorporating Art into the School or Therapeutic Milieu

KEVIN D. CAREY
School Art Therapist

AVVENTURA PRESS

Eynon, PA

Kevin Carey art photos by Mary Ann Capone
(Visit www.yessy.com to purchase artwork by Kevin Carey.)

Cover and interior design by Lee Sebastiani, Avventura Press

Library of Congress Control Number: 2008923067

ISBN-13: 978-0-9761553-2-4
Published by
Avventura Press
133 Handley St.
Eynon PA 18403-1305
570-876-5817
www.avventurapress.com

1st printing May 2008

Printed in the United States of America

Acknowledgements

Since my unfortunate automobile accident on March 7, 2001, I worked extremely hard to rehabilitate myself and alter my professional identity. I have lifelong "limitations," so learning ways to effectively deal with the limitations was very demanding and difficult at times, but I DID IT. I received a *great* deal of help and support from professors at Marywood University, former colleagues/friends at Pocono Mountain School District, my family and friends

Also, I would like to thank Lori Sebastiani, Lee Sebastiani, Debbie Murphy and Dr. Loree Guthrie for *everything* that they did, and continue to do, for me. In addition, I would give Barbara Parker-Bell, ATR-BC (director of graduate art therapy at Marywood University) credit for making this all possible. Because of Barbara's guidance and advice, I have become more "professional" and better prepared to make respectable contributions to society.

The entire experience at Marywood University has been absolutely wonderful. I met and established close friendships with many nice, helpful people during my tenure at Marywood University. The assistance and support that I received from Marywood University helped me become the man that I am today. It will never be forgotten.

Kid Artists Featured in Draw-Bridges

In October 2007, Karen Slachta, Children's Librarian at the Valley Community Library in Peckville, Pennsylvania, hosted an art workshop featuring some of the activities in *Draw-Bridges*. Avventura Press thanks Karen, the Library staff, and the dedicated kid artists (and their dedicated parents!) who participated. You can see examples of the children's artwork throughout this book.

Thanks to:

Kayla Bickauskas
Olivia Damski
Hannah Danielowski
Josh Danielowski
Kayla Davitt
Leanna Fuller
Lily Giovagnoli
Bruce Haines
Eleanor Haines
Maggie Haines
Alec Lukasik
Karleigh Lukasik
Logan Lukasik
Julia Mazur
Rachel Mazur
Vanessa Mazur
Mark Melesky
Nicole Melesky
Logan Munley
Matthew Nemeth
Jamie Roman
Alexander Slachta
Nathaniel Slachta
Jake Sweeney
Saige Sweeney
Laurelai Vanston
Alana Wright
Kayla Wright

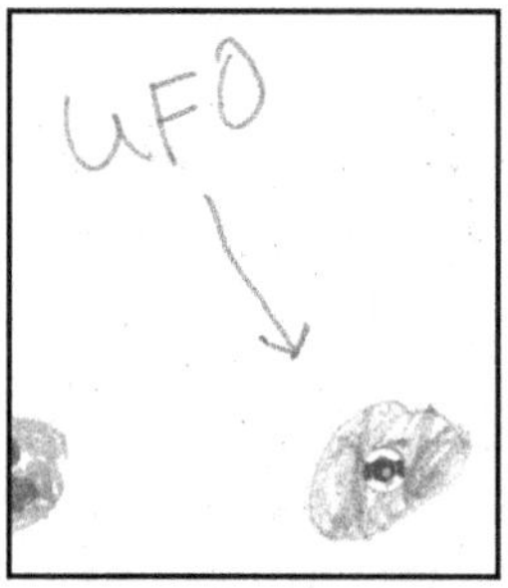

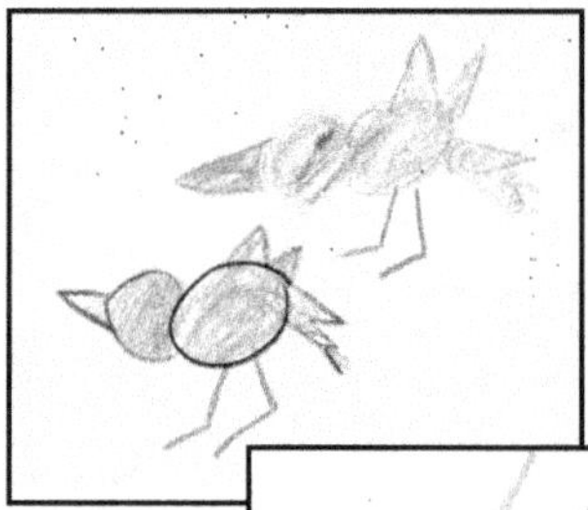

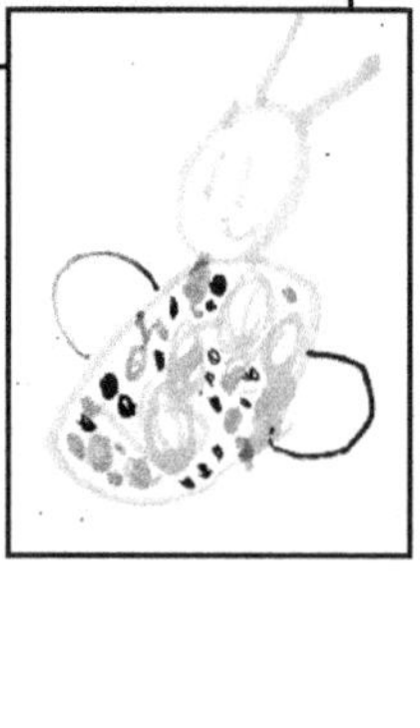

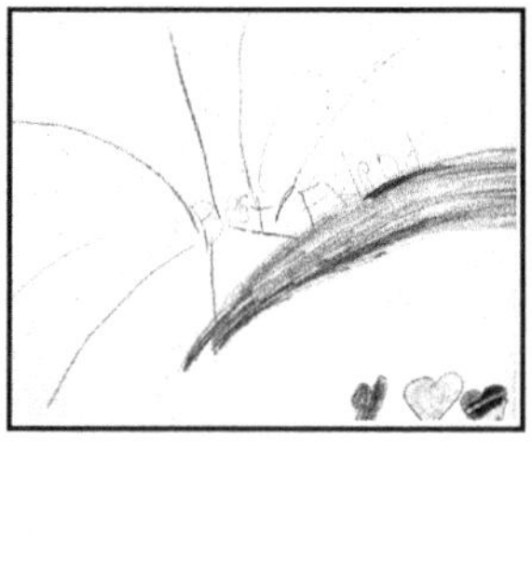

CONTENTS

Kevin Carey's Experience with Traumatic Brain Injury 2

Art Therapy and Children..............................27

Art in the Classroom 33

Activities..............................41

Behavior	43
Self-Expression	51
Family	69
Diversity	74
Miscellaneous Art Activities	78

Resources 83

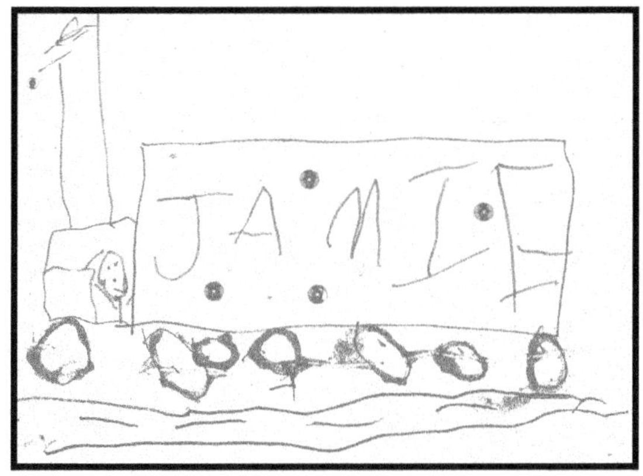

Part I
Kevin Carey's Experience with Traumatic Brain Injury

In theory there is no difference between theory and practice. In practice there is.

—Yogi Berra

Art therapy encourages personal growth and change. Art played an instrumental role in providing me with a new identity as, "Kevin the Artist/Art Therapist," after my automobile accident.

I'd like to give you a little bit of information about the head trauma I suffered and my interest in art. My career and future aspirations were abruptly delayed for almost *five* years. Let me explain what happened.

Kevin the Teacher

I was employed as a special education teacher in the Pocono Mountain School District (PMSD) in Northeast Pennsylvania. During the drive home after providing homebound instruction to one of my students, there was a horrific accident. A catastrophe occurred on March 7, 2001; the disaster almost ended my life.

It was snowing on that morning, so Clear Run Intermediate School had a two-hour delay. Pocono Mountain District was always one of the first schools to close or have delays because of its frequent heavy snowfalls. I can't remember anything of what happened on that day.

I chose to take my parents' Oldsmobile to work. Thank goodness I didn't take my Mustang...*thank God*!

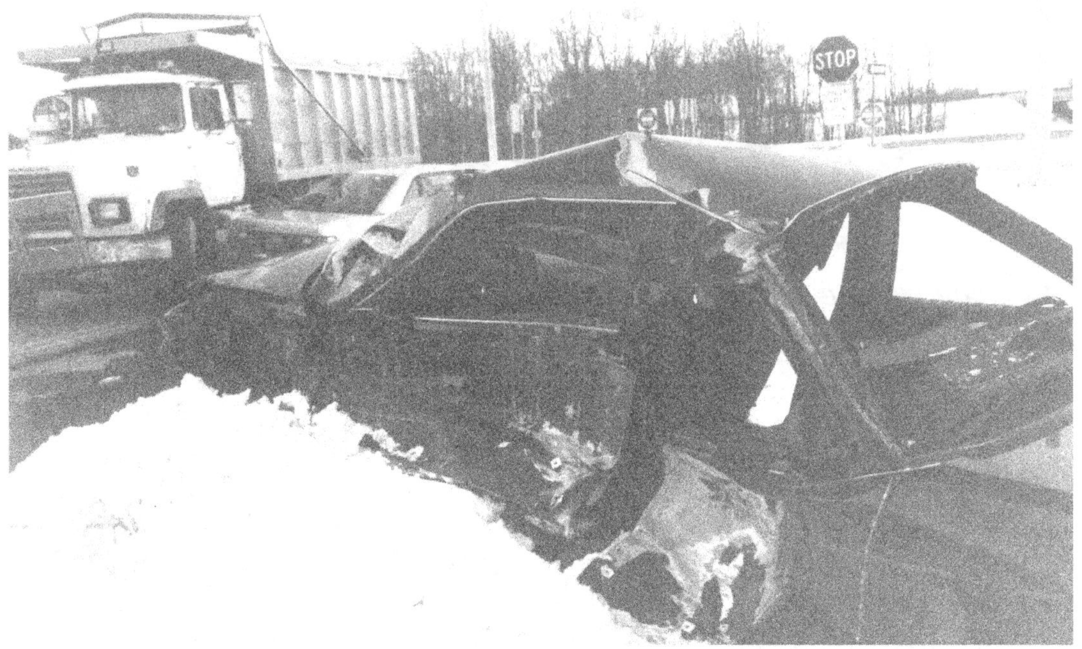

Kevin's car post-accident. Picture taken in 2001.

A dump truck hit me on the driver's side of my car and drove me for quite a distance after it hit me. The left side of my head smashed off the steering wheel causing a traumatic brain injury, I smashed my front teeth (they went through the skin below my bottom lip) and busted my chin; I sustained head trauma that resulted in my dominant right hand's becoming very unstable and unpredictable, among other injuries and *limitations.*

A helicopter transported me to Lehigh Hospital in Allentown because they have a trauma unit that specializes in accident victims. My body was mangled and the car was demolished. I am *very* fortunate to have survived the accident.

When I arrived at Lehigh Hospital I was in a coma, and I remained in a comatose state throughout my stay at Lehigh Hospital. After two months, I was moved to John Heinz Hospital in Wilkes Barre, Pa. I am very grateful to both Lehigh Hospital and John Heinz Hospital for the great job they did.

Initially after the accident when I awoke from the coma, I was a twenty four-year-old infant. I could not do *anything* on my own...NOTHING! *I couldn't even tie my shoelace!* I WAS COMPLETELY HELPLESS!

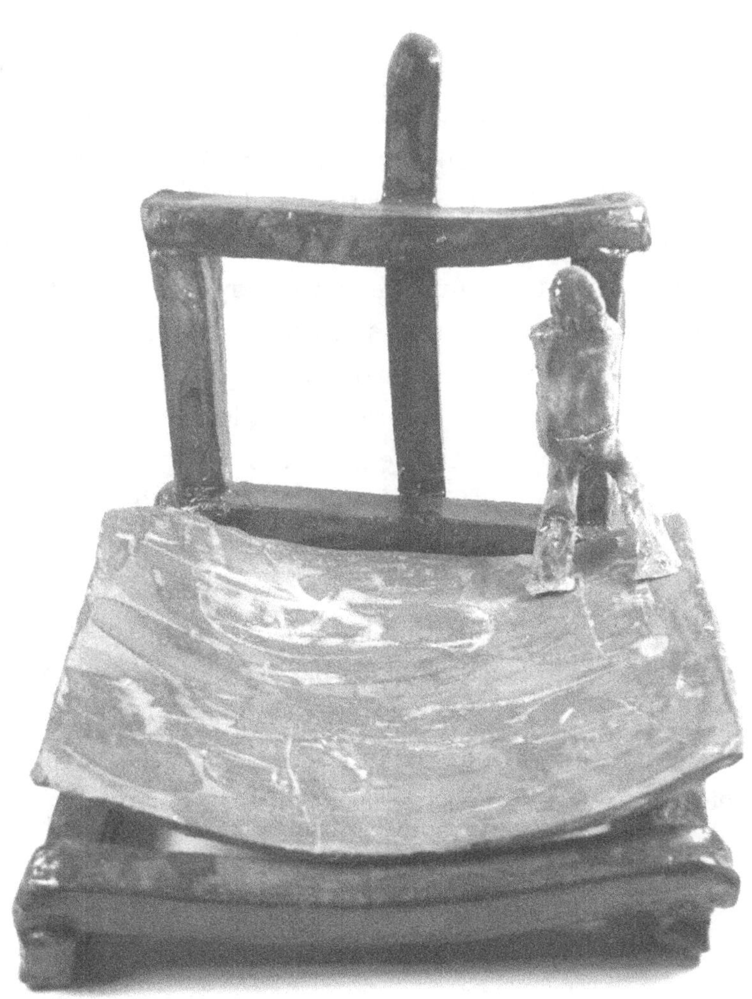

Trapped in a Personal Prison

Clay sculpture created by Kevin Carey in 2005. This sculpture/platter represents the way that I felt after my automobile accident.

Dexterity

I was employed as a special education teacher; however, my interest in art started when I was very young. I used to take art lessons when I was seven and eight years old. Back then everyone considered me a gifted artist...I used to *love* art!

Although I was talented a talented artist, I wanted absolutely nothing to do with art after I became an adolescent. *I don't know why.* My parents would occasionally bring up the subject of art in conversation. However, I was a stubborn know-it-all. They'd say, "What are you going to go for in college? Why don't you go for art?" I didn't even want to hear about it. Like some school kids, I thought that I knew *everything.* Looking back now, I knew *nothing.*

After my car accident, my writing could be fairly legible and my drawing was better than average when I *took my time.* The injury to my brain was on the left side of my head, so the right side of my body is affected. I couldn't, and still can't, complete any task that requires some precision and skill with my dominant right hand. The dexterity in my right hand did improve with time. However, it is still not even close to where it was before the accident. Now I am officially left-handed.

Like most people that have a disability (I prefer *limitation*), modifications and accommodations sometimes have to be made for me. With time and practice, practice, practice and more practice, I eventually became a successful *left-handed* artist.

I tried to do everything that I could to become better with my right hand. In an attempt to get my writing skills back, I was constantly drawing or sketching. Also, I wrote my name and the alphabet over and over and over again in my free time. I thought that would help, but it didn't.

Below I provide some samples of my right-handed artwork after my car accident:

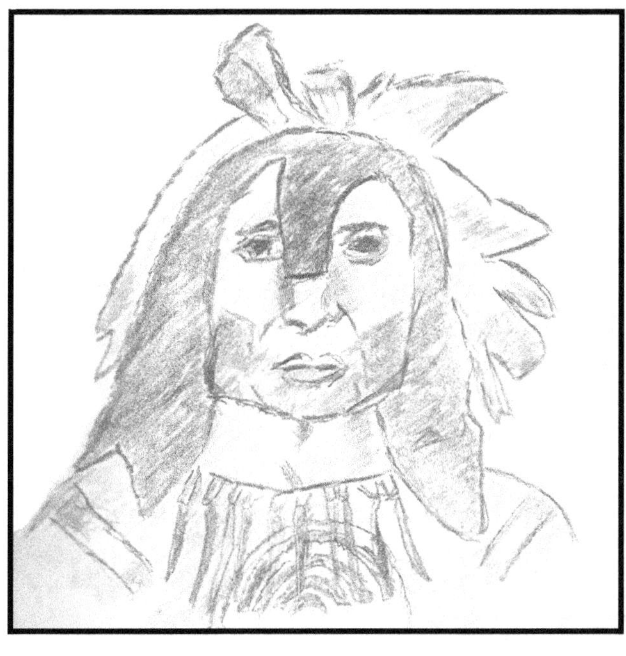

Indian man

Color pencil drawing, 2002.

Art Studio (perspective)

Color pencil drawing, 2003. This is probably the best picture that I did right-handed after my accident. It took ***days*** *to finish, and it is very special to me. Notice the Rolling Stones symbol on my easel.*

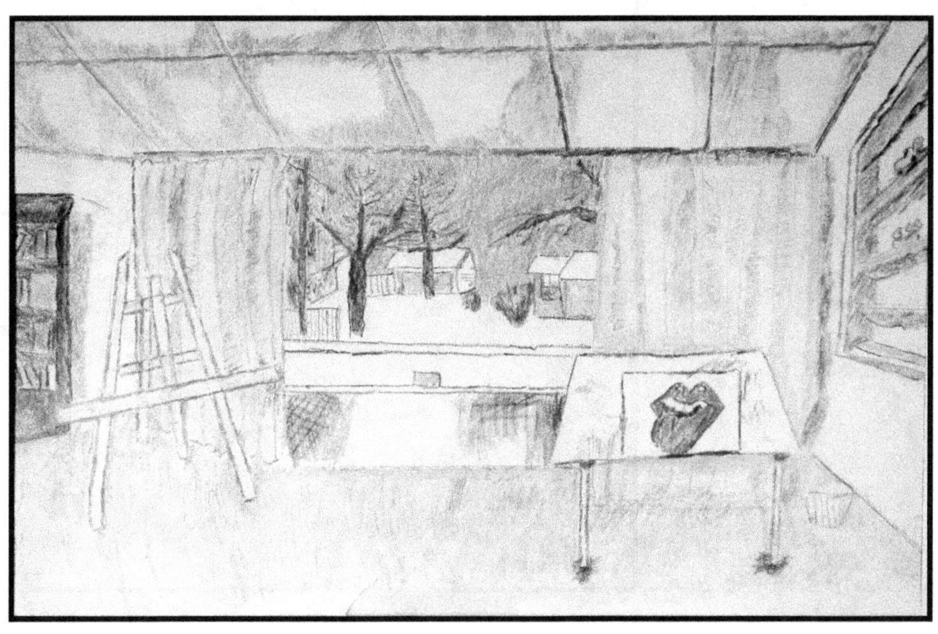

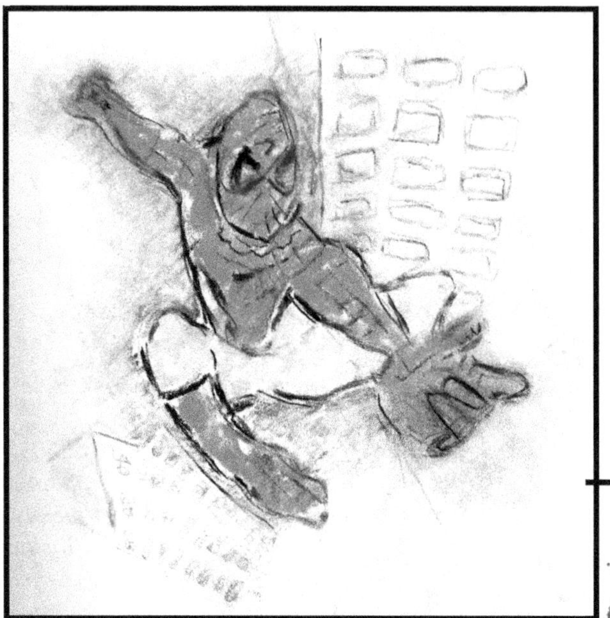

Spiderman

Pastel and charcoal drawing created by Kevin Carey in 2002

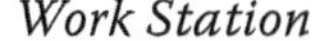

Work Station

Charcoal drawing created by Kevin Carey in 2002

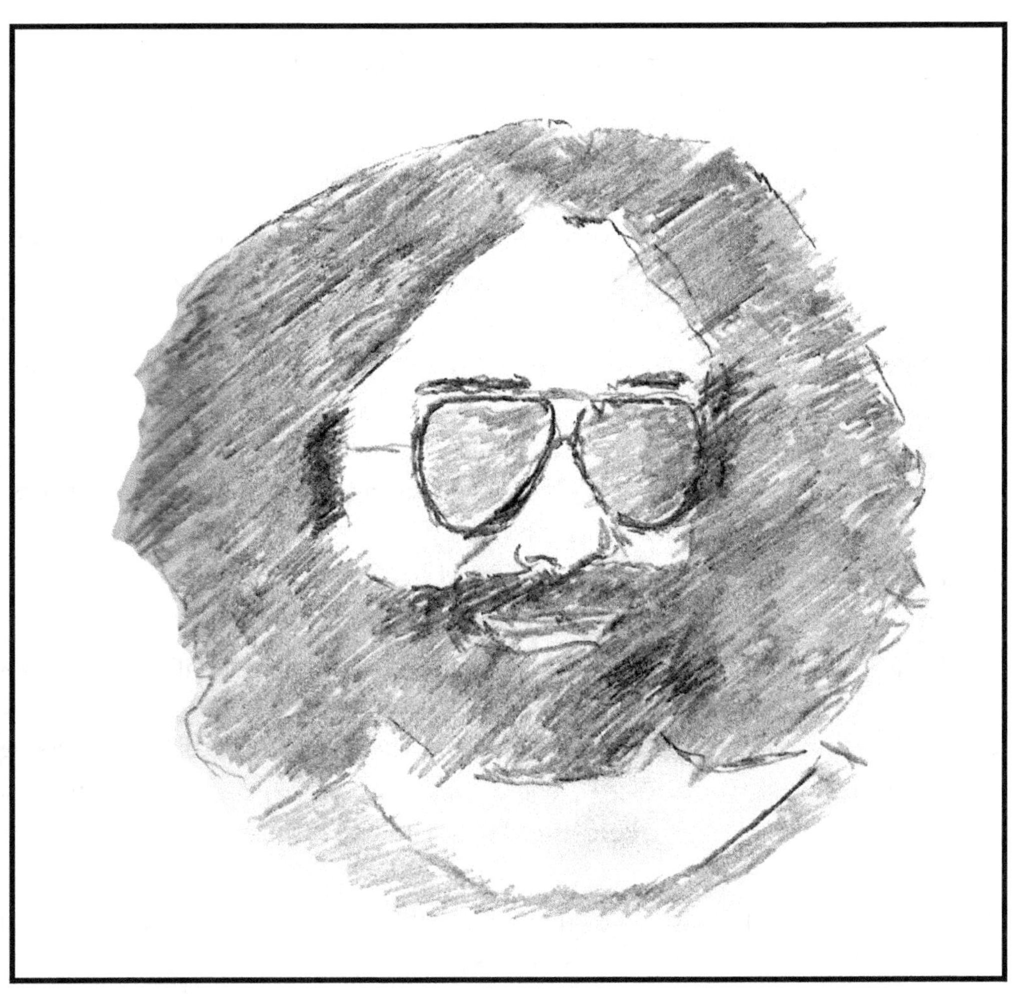

Jerry Garcia

Pencil drawing created by Kevin Carey in 2002. This is one of my better right-handed drawings after my accident; it took me hours to complete. (The lines in this drawing aren't very detailed, and like all of my post-accident drawing the picture is very sketchy.)

Things that would have been easy to draw or paint in the past were now extremely challenging for me because of my unpredictable right hand. I was a *much* better artist when I was eight years old.

Drawing and painting are far more difficult for me now, but creating art and helping people is what I truly enjoy doing. I feel that it is my purpose and reason for being involved in a horrific accident and surviving. Stuff happens, but *everything happens for a reason.* In my opinion, *everybody* is put on this earth to serve a purpose. At age 24, I discovered mine: I was meant to help people and inspire people through art....*That is my purpose.*

Marywood University's Art Department has an excellent reputation, so Marywood University is the place that I planned on going to school; Art Therapy was a major that I decided on. I had to teach myself to effectively manage my "limitations," and I had to learn everything about art *all over again.*

I chose Art Therapy as a major because I knew that I would be able to empathize with prospective clients, and I might even provide some inspiration. Actually, now I feel like crying when I come across someone with a physical or mental handicap. I became very sensitive and empathetic concerning disabled people... I get very sad and disturbed. *Those people could have easily been me.* I will never forget what my brother Mark told me. He said, "Kev, there is *always* someone worse off than you."

During my first semester at Marywood University, I was getting very, very frustrated. It would take me at least *six or seven hours* to complete a picture that would take the other students *one or two hours*; and their artwork was still *much* better than mine. I felt like a complete failure. I was getting very disappointed with school, and I was ready to give up. I would be practicing for hours and hours and hours, and quite frankly, I *STUNK.*

Revelation

My disposition changed a few weeks before the first semester at Marywood University ended.

My brother Mark and his future wife took me out to eat one night after school. I was explaining and/or *complaining* to them about the difficulty that I had with my right hand. I told them how I *could* create art, but I was extremely slow, difficult and far from impressive. After listening to me whine and complain for several minutes in the restaurant my brother Mark asked, "Does your left hand shake? Use your left hand." When I went home that night, I drew my first picture with my left hand. It actually came out all right! Although the picture is very special and *priceless to me,* I gave it to my brother Mark as a present. He wanted the "first left-hand drawing."

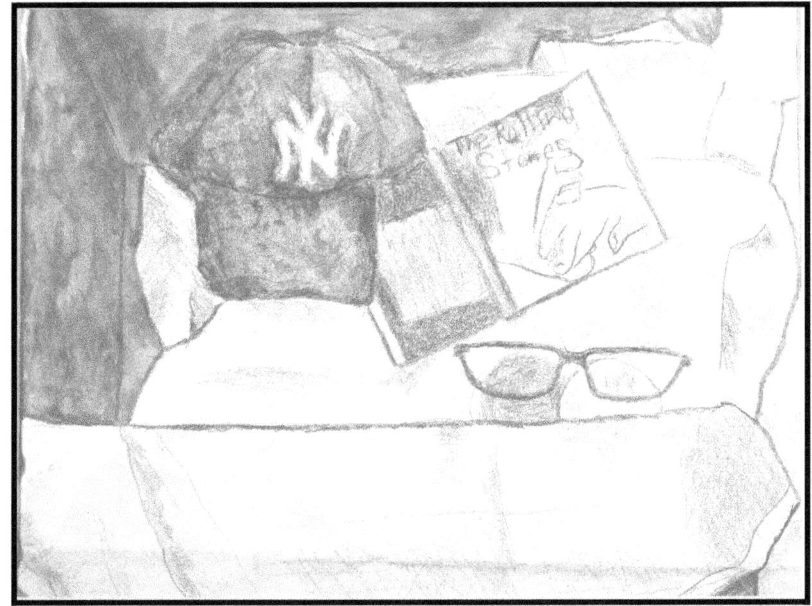

Sock Drawer

Watercolor and color pencil drawing

This is my first attempt at drawing left-handed. My left hand is my NON-DOMINANT *hand. For a school assignment, I had to draw a sock drawer with several items in it. The items contained in my drawer are "cool" to me. Notice that the Rolling Stones are in the picture.*

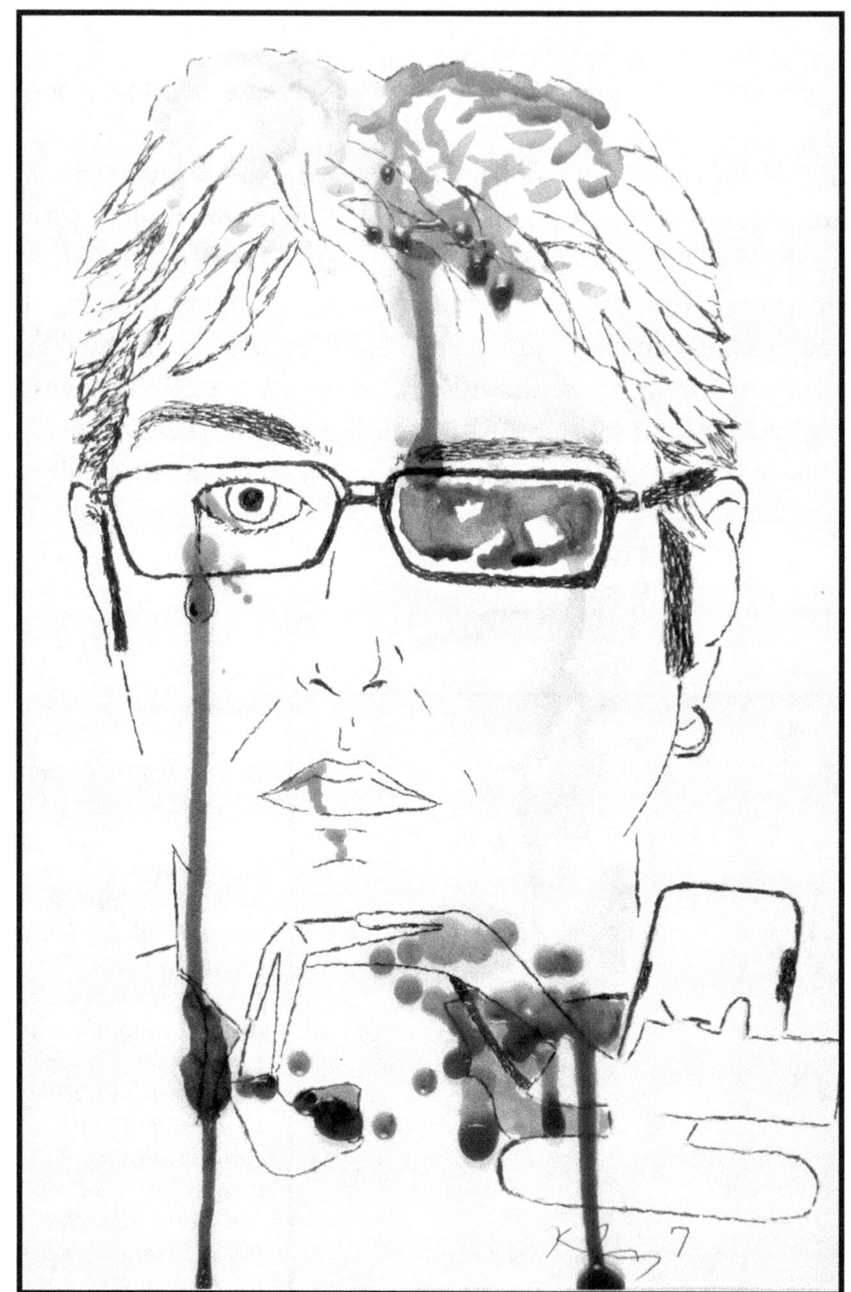

Kevin Carey continues to grow as an award-winning professional artist.

Self-Portrait
pen & ink, watercolor

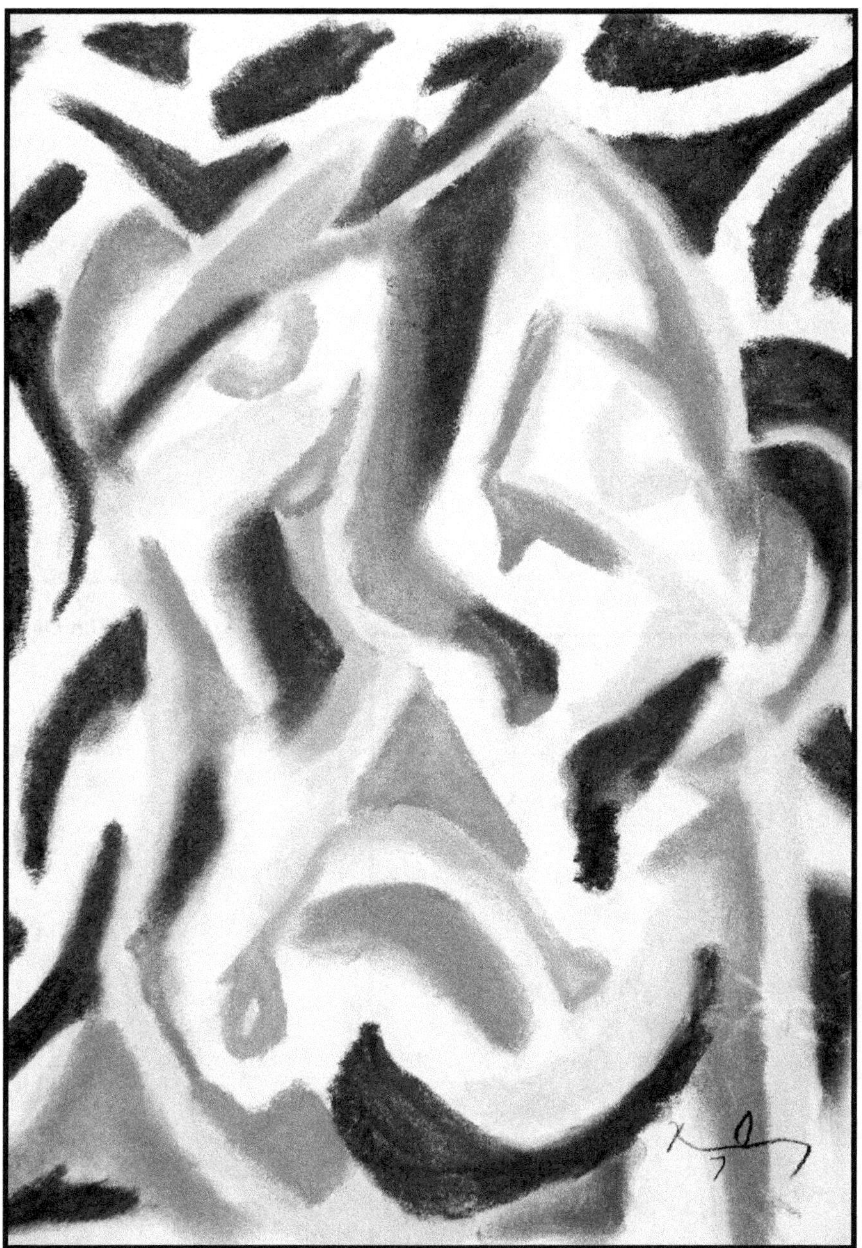

Blue

I was feeling blue and this pastel drawing is indicative of my feelings.

chalk pastels

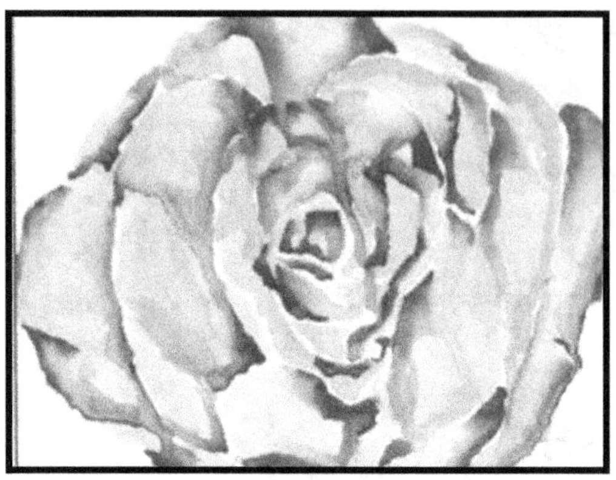

Purple Rose #2

This is a still life pcture of a rose. I used my imagination and made the rose purple.

watercolor

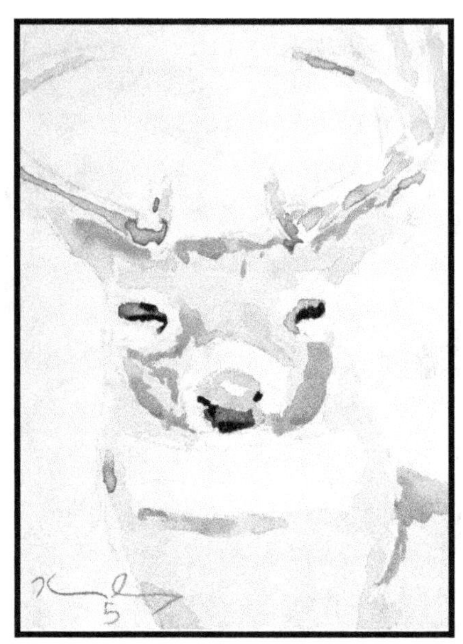

The Deer

This is a simple water-color of a deer.

watercolor

Ocelot

Only 100 ocelots are left in the US. I think it is a beautiful animal, so I copied a picture of one.

charcoal

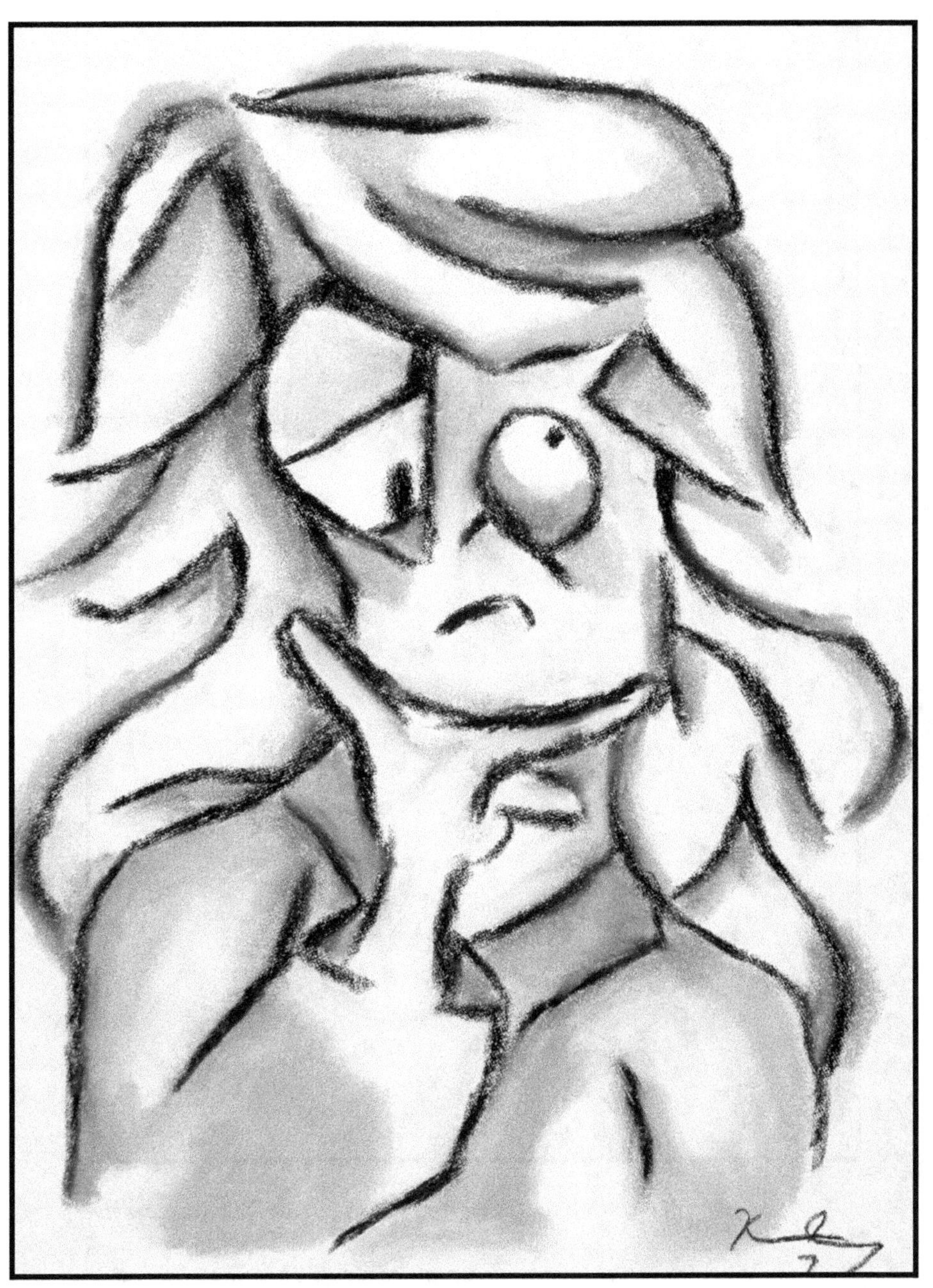

Stressed

This pastel drawing is indicative of the stress that I have in my life.

charcoal, chalk pastels

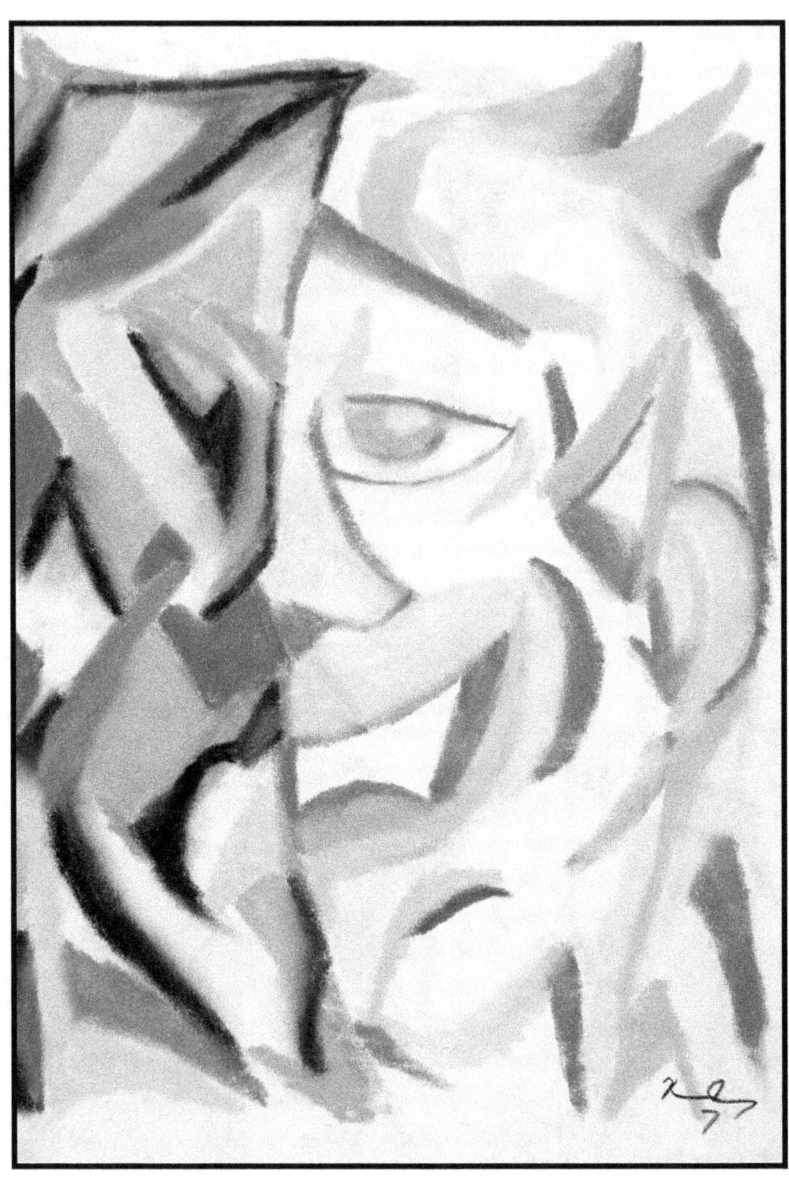

The New Perspective

My view on things changed quite a bit. This pastel drawing represents the two faces that I have/had.

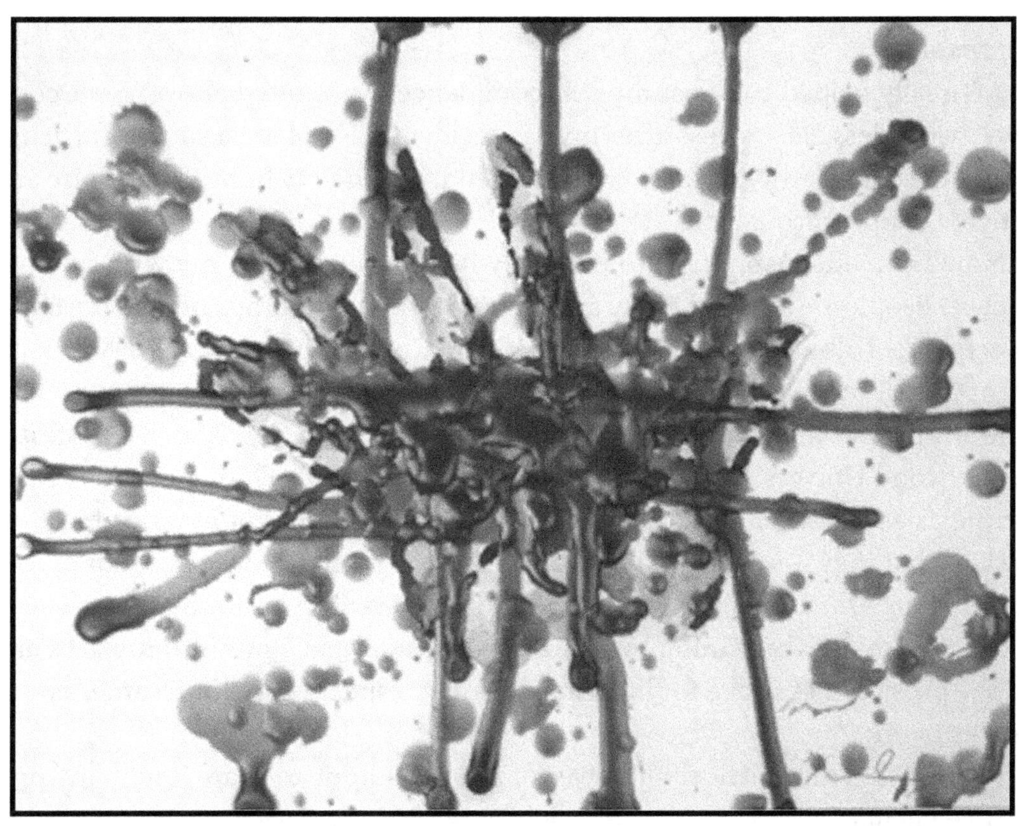

Sublimation

Sublimation means to direct repressed feelings. This is a black & white watercolor of a hand releasing those "feelings." The candle wax represents those "feelings."

watercolor, wax

Successes

Art really helped to boost my self-confidence. As I stated above, I felt completely worthless and useless after my car accident. Now, I am a successful artist, art therapist and author. I transcended my injuries, and my hope is to inspire and motivate people through art.

Now I provide inspiration to people, which in turn, helps me with *my* self-concept. People are amazed at my artistic ability, and numerous people purchase my artwork. To be completely honest, it is not even a big deal anymore that I taught myself to create art left-handed. I am a lefty....and that's it.

Many people, including my brother Mark and Stephen Garrison (art professor at Marywood University), told me, "Give it some time. You'll be fine. You're just starting as an artist." It took me about two years and *hours* of practice to refine my skills, but they were right. They were *absolutely* right because now I *am* "fine." I just had my *fifth* art show at B's Floral Shop in Scranton on June 1, 2007.

People are now beginning to realize the passion that I put into my artwork, and the passion that I have for life. Many people respect what I overcame, as well as my artwork.

I truly believe in the healing power of art, and I hope to share it with my prospective clients.

Assistant Superintendent of Pupil Services at Pocono Mountain School District, Dr. Loree Guthrie (former principal in the building that I taught in at PMSD), helped me a *ton*! Dr. Guthrie and I established a good rapport when I taught in her building. *She has a good heart.* When I inquired about an art therapy internship, she replied in an e-mail, "Kevin, you sound *wonderful.* Of course we can set up an internship for you!" I was delighted to read this e-mail! By the way, I later found out that Dr. Guthrie has a degree in Fine Art; *she is an ARTIST HERSELF!* The entire staff at PMSD has been *extremely* supportive of me, but Dr. Guthrie has been my main supporter.

Pocono Mountain did not have an art therapist at the time, so Dr. Guthrie ordered an abundance of art supplies out of *her own* budget. I was only an intern, but I had *a lot* more art supplies than some practicing art therapists. I know this for a fact. Everything worked out very well because my friend, Mrs. Deborah Murphy (former guidance counselor in the building where I taught), was now the Director of Guidance (head of the whole guidance department); like Dr. Guthrie, she believed in me, and the art therapy program that I trying to set up at PMSD. Debbie Murphy and Loree Guthrie are both *good* friends and *good* people.

I stayed at Pocono Mountain Junior High School (PMWJHS) for my third and fourth internship (the entire 2006–2007 school year). I was required to complete 400 hours for my third and fourth internships, but I enjoyed it so much I stayed at PMWJHS *well beyond* my required hours....I stayed for *the kids.* Waking up for work at 5:30 or 6:00 AM was *no longer* an arduous task.

At the beginning of the school year, I was introduced to Mr. Michael Loughney (a guidance counselor in PMWJHS). Mike was going to be my supervisor; we *immediately* hit it off. I consider myself very lucky to be working under the guidance of Mike. Mike is a *great* guy. When I informed Dr. Guthrie about this, she replied, "Great! I knew this would work!"

Kids were referred to me by the guidance staff, teachers, and principals. Toward the end of my stay at PMWJHS, I was seeing about fifty kids. The kids *absolutely* loved coming down to see me! They would seek *me* out. I would walk in, and the receptionist would say, "Joe was looking for you...And Lynne wanted to talk to you...Kristen asked where you were...Bobby said that he needed to see you...Tom asked about you...Bill came down to see if you were here a couple of times..."

I established an excellent rapport with the staff in the building and the kids that I saw for art therapy. The last day that I was at PMWJHS I said to the kids, "Pocono Mountain hired me to be a full-time art therapist in the district next year."

During my last day at PMWJHS (in May 2007), I asked the kids whom I worked with if they would write down some characteristics *about me* and/or *art therapy* that they liked and enjoyed. I was very touched by what they wrote.

"I enjoyed coming to see Mr. Carey because he is helpful, considerate, loyal, truthful and many more."

"I like coming down to Mr. Carey because he makes me laugh, and he is a funny person to be around."

"I like coming down to Mr. Carey because he is really cool and very fun. He is super nice to everyone and he helps us understand all sides of a problem. And he cheers me up when I am down."

"I like coming down to Mr. Carey because he is a good man. Also, he helps me to not get mad."

"I like to come down to Mr. Carey because we got to express ourselves through art."

"I like to go to Mr. Carey he always knows how to calm me down with art. It's like he brings out the little kid in me."

"I like to go to Mr. Carey because whenever I feel sad he helps me with my problems. Thank you Mr. Carey."

"Mr. Carey is awesome because he would do anything to help me out, and he's very funny. Overall he's a great guy!"

"To me, Mr. Carey is one of the coolest teachers because he listens and actually cares about what you say. And he really tries to do something about it."

"Mr. Carey didn't judge us, and he understood us better than any other adult could."

"Mr. Carey is a good listener and helped us with our problems. He is caring and supportive. I am glad that I got to come to him for advice and other things."

"Mr. Carey is a great listener. He has helped us with our problems. I am more relaxed now than I was before."

"I'm stubborn. I never really gave this amazing teacher a chance, but he never gave up on me. He is a great guy, and he understands teens better than most adults. He is funny and always makes sure you are okay. He is amazing, funny, caring, kind, and out of this world. I enjoyed coming to see Mr. Carey. He listened and understood. He expressed himself through his art and asked us to do the same."

"I enjoyed coming to see Mr. Carey. He let me express myself through art, and I find that great. It's fun and exciting to be in art therapy. He is a very caring person, and I hope to see him again.

If you are passionate and work hard at something, the hard work that you do will eventually pay off. I *truly* believe that. I actually made a difference in these kids' lives....THAT'S WHAT IT'S ALL ABOUT.

Dr. Guthrie asked me a few months ago, "Kev...what are you doing for the summer?" I said, "I don't know...why?" Dr. Guthrie said, "I would like for you to do art therapy part-time in summer-school with the kids." Needless to say, I did art therapy at PMSD in Clear Run Intermediate School (the former school where I taught) with the kids for the summer of 2007. The principal of Clear Run Intermediate, Mrs. Jessica Wenton (excellent teacher and former colleague), is extremely cool and very supportive; she often observes and even participates in my art therapy lessons. It is good to be working under two of my former colleagues at Clear Run Intermediate School: Mrs. Jessica Wenton (Principal) and Mrs. Karen Schito (Vice Principal). Numerous times, Jessica said to me, "The kids in this school can really use this."

Actually, for the 2007-2008 school year I am working in five schools in the Pocono Mountain School District. I am placed at Clear Run Intermediate School (CRIS), West Junior High School (WJHS), East High School (EHS), West Junior High School (WJHS) and Swiftwater Intermediate School (SIS).

The principal at Swiftwater Intermediate School, Mr. Tom Barbush, was one of the vice principals at Clear Run Intermediate School when I was a special education teacher. Don't forget, I hadn't seen Tom for *seven years.* Simply put, Tom is a terrific guy and welcomed me to his school with open arms. *But,* on the first day that I was scheduled at Swiftwater Intermediate School, I was sitting outside Tom's office waiting to talk to him. As I was waiting, Tom walked down the hall to his office, looked at me and very casually said, "Hello." When he got into his office (two seconds later), I heard, "O MY GOD.... *THAT* IS KEVIN CAREY. I DIDN'T EVEN RECOGNIZE HIM!" After he knew it was me, we talked for a while, and he told me that it was great to have me back.

Both Mrs. Donna Deluzio (Drug & Alcohol Counselor) and I are working directly with the Student Assistance Program (SAP team). We sometimes work together to advise a student how to deal with his or her issues. It is very fun, interesting and educational to be working so closely with Donna for a couple of reasons: 1. She is very sincere in helping the kids (as I am). 2. We make an effective team together. 3. I learn from her, and hopefully, she learns from me. 4. She is pretty funny.

Something happened at Pocono Mountain West High School that I would like to share with the reader....

I was doing art therapy with a student who has some very heartbreaking issues. At our initial meeting, I introduced the "feeling ball." The "feeling ball" is a colored ball (like a kick ball) that has the word *feelings* written across it. Basically, I ask the kids to share their feelings about whatever they would like to tell me (it is primarily used when we process artwork). Since this was our initial meeting, I used the "feeling ball" to get information about the student. I had the "feeling ball" in my hands first, so I shared my life as a teacher, my unfortunate accident, rehabilitation, limitations and accomplishments. I disclose personal information to my clients/students for one reason: It helps them to see what can be overcome.

Anyway, in our following session, the directive was *draw how you are misunderstood.* The student's drawing was extremely powerful, and he/she verbally expressed a ton of information. Then, the student told me, "You are not like the normal therapist...you know, suit buttoned up...asking me how *I feel* about this or that (the student demonstrated what he meant). *You are cool*...you got your shirt unbuttoned on the top and your chain is sticking out. You had to deal with stuff, and *you overcame it*." After our session was over, he shook my hand, and said, "Thank you." *It was very rewarding.*

Despite the fact that I am helping kids, I am *not* omnipotent....I wish that I were, but I am not. It took some time to accept, but I can't help *everyone* that I work with. I wish that I could help everyone, but that is not reality.

Part II

Why Use Art Therapy with Children?

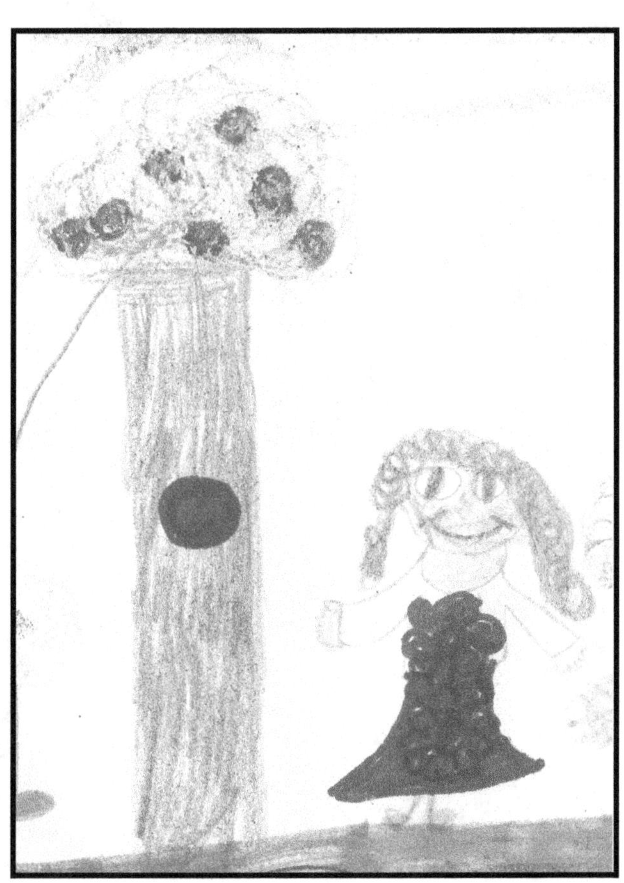

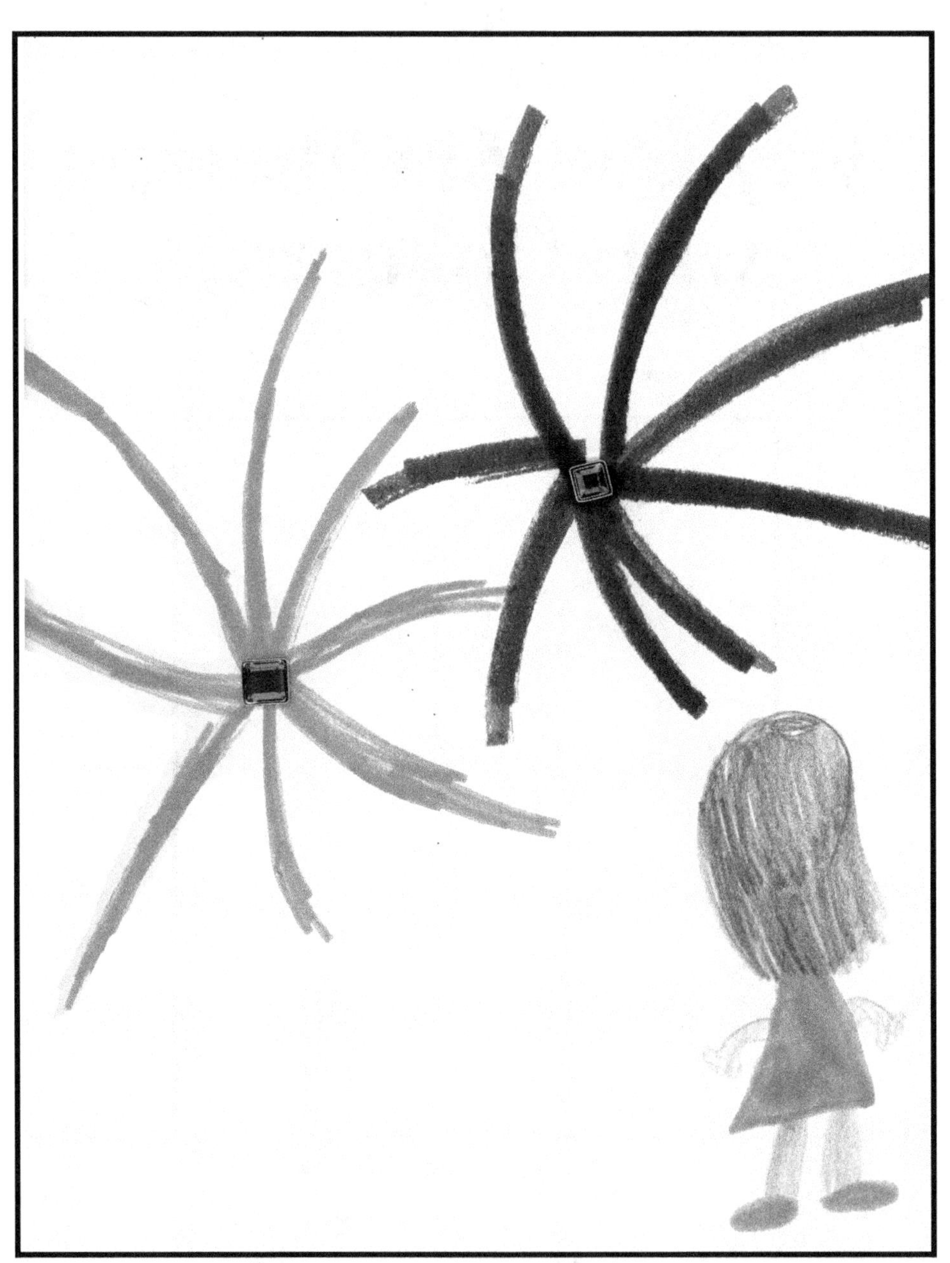

ART THERAPY is the therapeutic use of art making, within a professional relationship, by people who experience illness, trauma, or challenges in living, and by people who seek professional development. Goals of art therapy include relaxation, peer support, addressing feelings of isolation and addressing personal issues. These goals can be successfully accomplished by a creative and motivational therapist.

Cathy Malchiodi is one of the most highly-regarded children's art therapists in the field. She suggests that art expression has the potential to help children "open up" by making visible their thoughts, feelings, and perceptions through drawing, painting, and other art experiences. Opening up through self expression can encourage children to explore, release, and understand the source of emotional distress, ameliorate and alleviate trauma, and repair and resolve conflicts. Art therapy works well in helping children understand the reasoning why they feel a certain way and discover a new or different means of resolving their issues.

According to Ms. Malchiodi, children who express their secrets, traumas, and feelings to themselves and others have livelier immune responses, healthier psychological profiles, and far fewer incidences of illness. In addition, the benefits of achieving a sense of mastery are far-reaching: increased self-esteem, increased self-confidence, and the development of adaptive coping skills. The power of art expression helps children become more focused, seek interaction with others, and engage in meaningful self expression. Creative art approaches involving imagery and image making can have a positive effect on children's bodies, minds, and spirits.

Art therapist Jane Neilly Mallay says that expressive art exercises are goal-oriented, require no artistic skill, and help to process feelings and concepts without having to "say" every word. Children can permit their thoughts and feelings to emerge as they apply materials to the paper or canvas. It is the process, *not the product,* that is important.

Art therapy is not focused on a specific population; art therapy can be cathartic for *everybody,* even special-needs children with impaired verbal skills. Pioneering art therapist Helen Landgarten believes that an image is often more powerful than words, because images are more a basic, primitive form of communication than language. According to art therapist Harriet Wadeson, "We think in images. We had images before we had words."

Art therapy offers the excitement of exploring a person's individuality and creativity. Creating an image on paper to express a feeling is undeniable proof of an individual's existence and uniqueness, and can serve as a powerful boost to children with low self-esteem.

Art Therapy in Schools

Dafna Moriya is a well-known advocate of art therapy programs in school settings. She observes that an ever-increasing number of districts are hiring staff art therapists. They collaborate with teachers, counselors, and other staff to encourage students to work toward goals shared by art therapy and education: problem solving, organizational skills, stress reduction, enhancing self-esteem and self-confidence through mastery, and learning codes for acceptable behavior.

Ms. Moriya suggests that just being involved in art benefits children, including children with special needs, on the cognitive level. Art therapist Judith Aron Rubin lists such cognitive skills as attention, planning, concentration, symbolization, and decision-making; group art activities foster social skills through sharing supplies and providing peer feedback.

Art Therapy and the Classroom Teacher

Art teachers and classroom teachers can enhance artmaking as a therapeutic experience, according to Peggy Dunn-Snow and Georgette D'Amelio, art teachers and art therapists. They suggest several ways in which art teachers (and by extension, classroom teachers who include artmaking as an activity in the school day) can make a positive contribution to the wellbeing of their students:

1. Teachers can talk empathetically to their students about their art. Children will know that an adult cares about them and their artwork, which always has a purpose and a meaning to the child. Questions about the *overt* content ("Describe what you see in your drawing") and the *associative* content ("Tell me about the feelings, memories, wishes, or dreams your painting reminds you of") help children define their artwork's subject matter and themes. It is important to avoid imposing your own adult interpretation of the art.

2. Teachers can provide the appropriate level of structure for their art assignments. For example, children with learning disabilities, ADHD, or mental retardation may benefit from directions presented in specific steps as they master a new art task. A non-directive approach and more complex art assignments may be more appropriate for students with higher levels of cognitive, emotional and social skills.

3. Teachers can collaborate with school art therapists, counselors and school psychologists to develop artmaking activities to meet the individual needs of students. In the May, 2000 issue of *Art Education*, Ms. Dunn-Snow and Ms. D'Amelio suggest that this gives students "a safe, socially acceptable, and alternate way of expressing their needs, concerns, hopes and fantasies."

IMPORTANT CAUTIONS: Ms. Dunn-Snow and Ms. D'Amelio strongly recommend that teachers alert parents or a counselor if a student creates a disturbing graphic image. This may be the first step in recognizing and addressing a potentially serious problem. Also, they caution teachers to avoid talking to students about the *latent* level of content in their artwork. This is the level dealing with unconscious content, and it should be left to trained art therapists to engage in this type of dialogue with children.

Reference:

How Art Teachers Can Enhance Artmaking as a Therapeutic Experience: Art Therapy and Art Education. Peggy Dunn-Snow, Georgette D'Amelio. *Art Education*, Vol. 53, No. 3, Dialogue (May, 200), pp. 46-53

Art Therapy and Parents

Parents who would like to share creative expression with their children are encouraged to explore the art activities in this book. (But please read the caution above!)

Part III

Integration of Art Into the Classroom and Therapeutic Milieu

Advice from an Art Therapist and Special Education Teacher

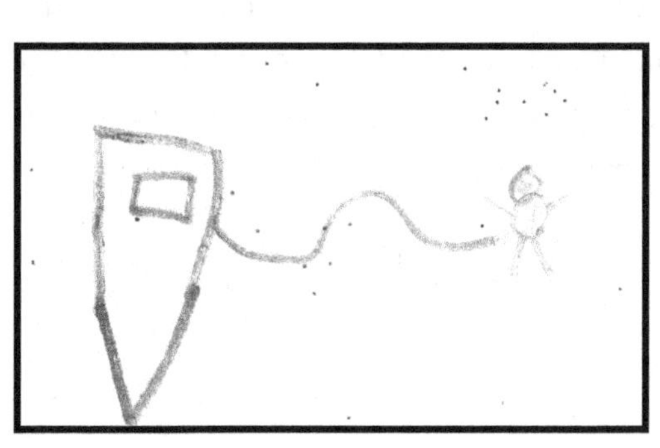

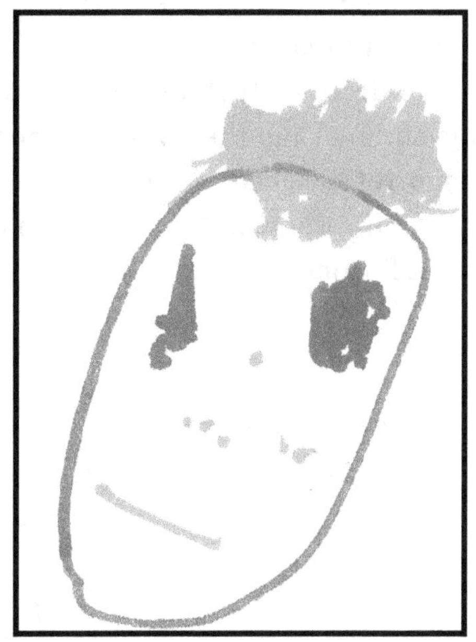

From the Heart

First of all, I would like to thank everyone who purchased this book and took the time to read it. Also, I would like to extend my sincere gratitude to everyone that supported me and help me to become the man who I am today.

The events that took place in my life took a lot away from me; however, they also gave me a lot in return. Nowadays when I come across someone with a physical or mental handicap it affects me in a deep and personal way. Like most people, I felt bad before my car accident, but anymore I get extremely, extremely disturbed. I am very fortunate that I survived the accident only with the minor limitations that I now have.

I feel that being involved in a near-fatal car accident makes me a better therapist. I can empathize and understand exactly what it is that my clients/students are dealing with....The kids that I work with understand this, and they respect me for this reason.

I understand that my behavior and therapeutic techniques are somewhat unconventional, but they work for the vast majority of kids. I have many friends and supporters at Pocono Mountain School District that helped me to get "my foot back in the door," but I worked very hard inventing myself as a school art therapist at Pocono Mountain School District. *Thanx.*

From my experience working as an art therapist at Pocono Mountain School District (PMSD), I *know* rapport with students is imperative for the therapy to work. When they like and respect you, they are *a lot* less resistant and more likely to open up.

The purpose of this book is to give educators *and* art therapists ideas and ways in which art can be incorporated in sessions and/or classrooms. In my professional opinion, art will allow teachers to plan interesting lessons that will keep students willing to learn. Personally, I incorporate teaching in most, *if not all*, of my art therapy sessions because I have a degree in elementary/special education; I have much classroom experience, and before my accident, I was a teacher. I almost always do an introduction as an anticipatory set in order to make the participants *excited* about the art activity.

It is important to remember that "art" encompasses many different things such as painting, drawing, writing, sculpture, poetry, acting and music. All of these modalities can be integrated into the regular education curriculum in order to make kids *excited* about learning. I sometimes incorporate music in the art activity, but music is always playing while art is created in my room...ALWAYS. I am only thirty-one years old, but sometimes I forget that the kids that I work with are *at least* fifteen years younger than me. I'll share a humorous story that happened during one art therapy session at Clear Run Intermediate School.

Once I said to a student, "John, do you want to hear music?" I was playing air guitar and dancing like Mick Jagger when I asked him. He smiled and said, "Yep!" I said, "Cool! What about the Rolling Stones?" He replied, "Okay....Who is *that*?" I said, "You know...Mick Jagger?" I strutted like Mick, jumped around like him, pointed like him. You know, acting like Mick. The student looked at me like I was nuts, and said, "Who??? Who's Mick Jagger?"

When I was working as an intern in a hospital with certified art therapist Kim Hayden, she once recommended, "Kevin, *break down the task*. You should tell the clients, 'Okay do this...When you are done do this...Next do this...'" Kim was absolutely correct because the clients sometimes get confused when the directive is complicated.

From my experience working with kids, I came to make a few observations about keeping kids well-behaved and motivated. The first is that it's effective to establish one to three rules in the teaching or therapeutic milieu that can encompass many things (e.g. *Be Respectful*). In my professional opinion, *too* many rules become too complicated for the kids.

In my art therapy room, I have *one* rule...ONE. The one rule is RESPECT. I spend the first half of the session discussing exactly what *respect* means. I will ask questions such as, "What does respect mean to you? How can you be respectful? How can you be respectful of my art supplies?" I'll throw a pencil across the room and say, "Is this respectful? Why? How can you be respectful of me?"

Five kids and I went outside in early summer to use sidewalk chalk. My directive was: *Draw what you enjoy about school.* One of the students threw a piece of sidewalk chalk to another student. Another member of the group saw this and said, "Hey John! What do you think you're doing? RESPECT the art supplies!" As long as the kids or participants fully understand your rule(s), problems will be kept to a minimum. When kids come to see me for art therapy, they *almost* never disobey my ONE rule. But as I said, *some* students are reluctant to listen to anyone.

The facilitator should be honest with kids and treat them like *adults.* Kids are kids; however, that doesn't mean we should patronize them. Children are *much* smarter and more perceptive than we sometimes give them credit for. They will have much more respect for you if you are up front and honest with them.

In my professional opinion, it is important for the therapist/teacher to joke and have fun with kids, but remember, *YOU* are the adult and you are responsible for the kids. *You* are the adult and need to model appropriate behavior. It is imperative that the group leader or teacher *always* take the child's or anyone's perspective into consideration. In sum, *listen* to what people have to say about something.

In addition, the teacher/art therapist *always* should be enthusiastic. I truly love what I do, and the kids can easily see this. I am very energetic when I am explaining the directive, and I am very excited about seeing them participate. I am excited about the kids' artwork, and their participation in the group. The kids love my enthusiasm, which in turn, makes them *very* ready, willing and excited about participating in the activity.

When the kids walk into my art therapy room, I'll say, "THERE'S ANNIE!" or "HERE'S KRISTEN!" or "CHARLIE! THERE'S THE MAN!" One student at PMWJHS said, "I *never* had a teacher like you." I asked, "What do you mean?" The student said, "I never had a teacher as excited and enthusiastic as you....Most of my teachers just yell."

Some renowned art therapists claim that they NEVER create their own artwork in art therapy sessions with clients. I can respect and understand their perspective, but I don't share this belief. I know I am fairly new to the profession, but I believe that my contentions are well-supported.

Personally, when possible, I feel that it is important to make art along with the clients. I admit, *sometimes* it is not feasible for the art therapist to make artwork with clients because of regulations and paperwork. I know this. Also, clients may need help with *their* artwork or the art therapist must supervise their activity. However, *if* the art therapist does make art with the clients, it can yield some very positive outcomes.

I will argue against some common reasons for NOT making artwork with clients. My purpose is not to disrespect the art therapists who do not make art with their clients in art therapy sessions. However, I will back up my reasons for participating in art activities. I have personal experience to support my beliefs. Some common reasons for NOT making art with the clients are:

1. The art therapist should give his or her full attention to the client.

I agree that the client should come first. However, making art alongside the client can inspire and motivate him/her to experiment with different media.

Also, it demonstrates exactly what is expected of the client (at times clients do not fully grasp the directive). I *always* ask clients if they like my suggestions. The art therapist can say, "I think your picture would look really cool if you did this in your picture." Some responses that I have heard are: "Wow, that's cool!" "Awesome!" "That is sooo neat!" The clients respond, "Thank you, Mr. Carey!"

2. The client may be intimidated by the art therapist's artwork.

From my experience, that statement is completely untrue. NEVER once have I heard a client say, "No, I don't want to do this. YOU are too talented an artist!" The art therapist's artwork will give clients new methods and ideas which will enhance their creativity.

A few times my kids (clients) said, "WOW! That is really good!" I said, "Thank you, I appreciate it. I am a professional artist." That was it. It was never brought up again. From my standpoint, art therapists should be *good artists.* Just as music therapists are typically good musicians, or industrial arts teachers are typically good carpenters, or karate instructors are typically martial arts experts, art therapists should be expected to be good artists.

3. Art therapists should NOT project their feelings/problems on the clients.

I agree that art therapists should not project their problems onto the clients. It should be all about the clients. However, demonstrating that problems are prevalent in everyone helps them to realize that they are *not alone.* I have absolutely no problem disclosing personal information about myself if it helps the clients deal with their issues. I am an adult and the group leader, but just as the participants do, I have issues that I have had to deal with. It will show them that I'm not really different. In my life, I have had many problems that I overcame, and I tell clients how I dealt with and/or transcended my issues. This gives them support and advice in dealing with their own issues.

It is important to note that I am not taking credit for the art activities that are outlined below. Many of the art activities are derived from the readings of talented and creative practicing art therapists and the wonderful art therapy staff at Marywood University. I will never forget what Kim Hayden, ATR-BC (certified art therapist and professor at Marywood University) said to me. When I was Kim's intern, she said, "I have an idea of what I want to do, but first, I see where the clients are at on a specific day. I spontaneously come up with an art task based on their feelings." In addition to Barbara Parker-Bell, ATR-BC (director of Graduate Art Therapy at Marywood University), Kim was an excellent and creative instructor/supervisor; many art activities that I do are derived from the ideas of Kim Hayden and Barbara Parker-Bell.

Examples of activities are not provided because *everyone* will have their own interpretations of the art. Quite possibly, teachers or therapists will develop their own variation of the activities that I have listed. Art therapy is about expression, so an art therapist should never critique the quality of a client's artwork. Remember, art is *always* in the eye of the beholder.

However, the ideas are *only* ideas. They can easily be changed, modified and embellished to effectively meet the needs of the target population. Also, PMSD did provide me with many art supplies, and I realize that many parents and professionals do not have access to these supplies. But numerous other materials can be used in their place in order to make the task successful. You can find inexpensive art supplies at www.orientaltrading.com.

The following activities may take more than one typical class period to complete. Two or even three or four periods may be necessary.

Below is an activity that requires more than one period to complete:

Anger Mountain

1st session: We will have a group discussion about what makes us angry (I want the clients to talk about trivial things). I'll talk about my disgust with mayonnaise.

Then, I will talk about serious things that make me angry (ignorance, disrespect). I will ask the clients to represent things at home and in school that make them angry.

Carving tools and 3 or 4 hard foam blocks (available at Dick Blick) will be distributed to each client.

For the remainder of the session, clients will be encouraged to write words, draw symbols, and draw pictures onto the foam blocks with the carving tools.

2nd session: The group will continue carving into their foam blocks. When they are finished, they will be encouraged to put them together to form a "mountain." A hot glue will be used to hold the foam pieces together.

3rd session: Clients will be encouraged to put the final touches on their "mountains" and paint them with acrylic paint. Finally, we will have a group discussion (process) about the "mountains."

Part IV

Activities

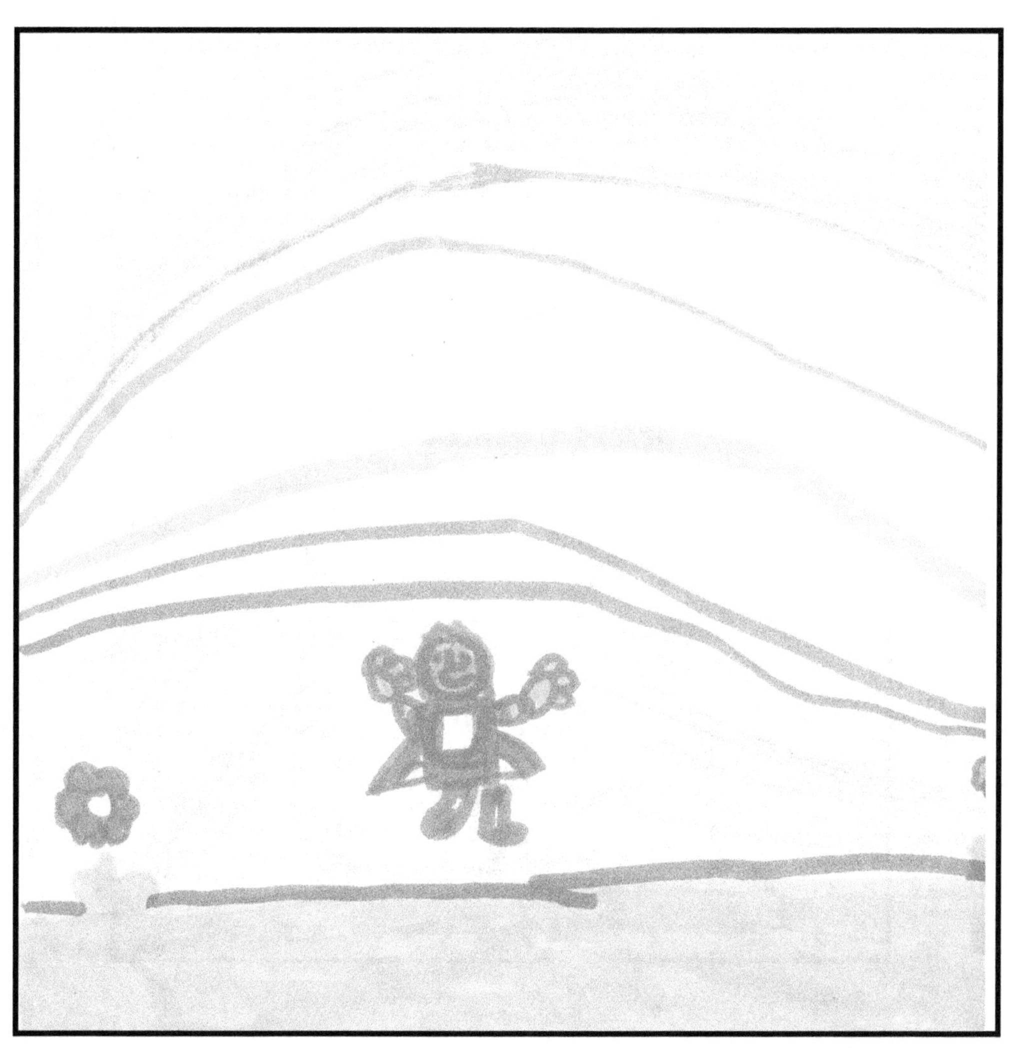

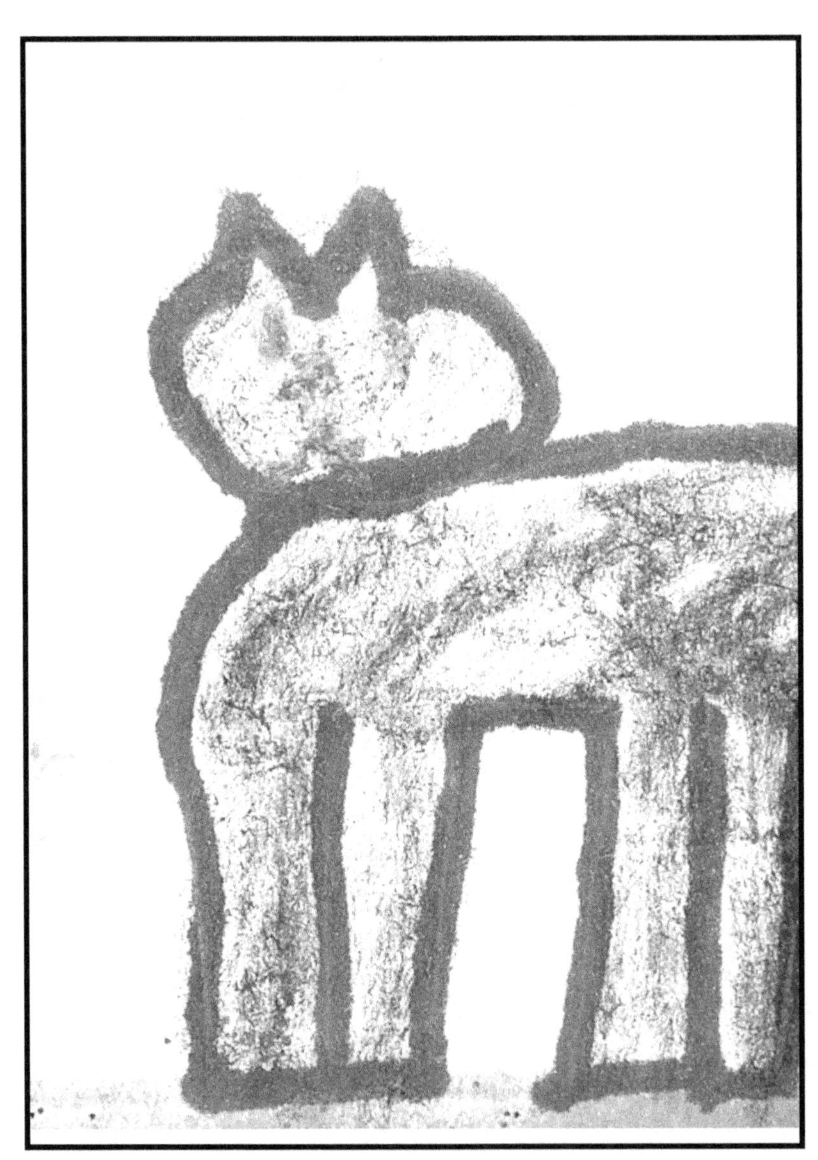

Activities Concerning Behavior

Idea #1

Respect

This is recommended for the first activity.
The goal for this activity is for students to comprehend what constitutes respectful behavior.

1 The group leader will write the words "RESPECT" in BIG bubble letters on a sheet of paper.

2. The students will be encouraged to color/draw pictures, symbols or words that are representative of the concept of respect. The group facilitator can remind the students to be as creative as possible.

3. Finally, a large mat (if available) could be placed around the picture. It could be hung on the wall, and then can be talked about by the group.

OR group members can be allowed to draw or paint a picture of respectful behavior individually on a sheet of paper (the pictures of respect can be hung around the room).

Idea #2

ABCD (Theory of Emotional Disturbance)

The goal is for students/clients to change their beliefs about a situation into more realistic and appropriate thinking and actions. A great deal of teaching can be done to prepare for the art activity.

This was taught to me in the Marywood Counseling Center by Mrs. Barb Decker.

1. On the board, the teacher writes examples of A—Activating Event suggested by students (e. g. failed a test). Next, the students can identify their B—Beliefs About (e.g. anger, frustration, depression). Then, C—Upsetting Emotional CONSEQUENCES (e.g. annoyance: I am upset that I did poorly on the test, but now I know to study harder). Next is D—Disputing of Irrational Ideas (e.g. Failing one test does not mean that I am a failure).

2. Next, students identify a New Emotional Consequence (e.g. it is annoying to fail a test, but that doesn't mean that I will be a failure).

3. Then, on the board, the teacher/facilitator can address several issues brought up by the group. The ABCD Theory of Emotional Disturbance can be used in an attempt to modify counterproductive thinking.

OR students can pick blindly from a stack of prepared situation cards (e.g. boyfriend found another girlfriend).

Idea #3

Inappropriate Behaviors

The group will identify some behaviors about themselves that have to be changed.
Activity derived from Kim Hayden, ATR-BC

1. As an opening, the group will discuss inappropriate behaviors by celebrities. Next, small pieces of wood (e.g. craft sticks) will be distributed to all of the group participants. They will identify "bad" behaviors about themselves that should be improved. The group participants will use acrylic paint to write the words on the craft sticks (e.g. MAD, IMPATIENT, RUDE).

2. While the paint dries on the wood, the group will construct a "fire" from mixed media. When the "fire" is finished, one by one, the participants will place the wood on the fire.

3. As group members add to the fire, they will say how and why they want to dispose of the behavior.

Idea #4

Abstract Plaster Sculpture of Anger

The goal for this activity is to allow the student/client to express anger or frustration in a acceptable and more appropriate manner.

1. First, the participants can be shown images of abstract sculptures. As a group, the meanings of the sculptures can be discussed.

2. Containers to hold the plaster can be distributed (empty milk cartons would work fine). Group members mix Plaster of Paris with water until smooth. Then, the plaster can be used to fill their containers. While plaster is drying, participants could be introduced to carving tools and safety. *Protective glasses and gloves should be distributed to protect the participants' eyes and hands.*

3. After plaster is dry, the container can be removed from it. Group members will be allowed to work freely on the plaster sculpture. *However, the group leader should carefully supervise the participants to avoid injuries.* Finally, when the group is finished a discussion can be held among group members.

OR students can carve or scrape words that indicate *anger* into the plaster. The students will be allowed to use a thesaurus to assist them.

Idea #5

PROPER BEHAVIOR

The goal of this activity is to teach students/clients about the appropriate way to interact with someone.

1. The group facilitator should act and provide examples of the three ways that people interact with one another: *AGGRESSIVE, NON-ASSERTIVE,* and *ASSERTIVE.* Body pose, voice inflection, eye contact, and negative/positive words should be addressed by the group facilitator; the facilitator will demonstrate each one of these ways with volunteer participants from the group.

2. The clients/students will be asked to demonstrate ASSERTIVE behavior given a situation (e.g. interaction with parents, conflict with another person or boy/girl issues, giving and receiving criticism).

3. Then, a discussion can be held among the group members concerning the behavior.

OR the participants can be encouraged to draw or paint a situation in which they acted aggressively or non-assertively.

Idea #6

Negative Behaviors

The goal is for the students/clients to be able to vent their anger in a positive manner.

1. A wood burner can used to burn negative words/ways students sometimes act (e.g. MEAN, NASTY, RUDE) onto various pieces of scrap wood. Students can also scrape or carve the behaviors into pieces of wood.

2. A garbage box (collaboratively constructed by the clients) will be placed before the group.

3. Finally, the group facilitator should ask the participants what they would like to do with the "box of negative words." They can bury it, throw it in the trash, stomp on it, or whatever.

OR a collaborative sculpture can be created by group members. Group participants will talk about their behaviors with the group leader.

OR a personal box can be constructed by each group member individually to contain the "negative behaviors."

Idea #7

Deconstructing the Wall

The goal for this activity is the recognition of the issues that must be overcome in order to act appropriately.

1. As an opener, the teacher or therapist will suggest several issues (4-5 issues) that the student must deal with on a regular basis.

2. Next, the student will be asked to mold enough clay blocks to cover a piece of wood (the wood piece should be about 4" x 4"). The student will write a word on each clay block (e.g. arguing).

3. While the clay blocks are drying, the student(s) will paint a *positive* word or symbol on the wood.

4. Finally, the clay blocks will be laid on the wood. When the student acts appropriately *instead* of engaging in the negative behavior, he/she will remove the clay block from the wood. Students will keep removing clay blocks until the painting underneath is revealed.

Idea #8

Self-Injurious Behavior: Body Part Tattoo

IMPORTANT: This activity should be led by a professional therapist only. The goal for this activity is to replace self-injurious behaviors with a constructive art activity.

1. Clients will place plaster strips over the injured area to create a mold. They will let the mold harden and remove it from the area (e.g. forearm or calf).

2. When it dries, the client will replace the mold over the self-injured area. The client will use acrylic paint to paint whatever is on his/her mind onto the molds.

3. When it is finished and dry, the therapist will help the client glue the mold onto a piece of wood with a hot glue gun. Then, the art therapist and client can talk about the created art.

OR clients will be asked to place plaster strips over any part of their body that is "hurting." They will be encouraged to paint their feelings about the "injury."

OR clients will be given a lump of self-hardening clay. They will sculpt a body part which they self-mutilate (i.e. cut). Then, the clients will be allowed to use clay tools to scrape, dig or cut into the molded piece. When the clay dries, the will paint the body part however they chose to.

Idea #9

Marijuana/Alcohol Abuse Information

The goal for this activity iis the students to become aware of the symptoms of drug abuse.

1. First, an informative discussion about marijuana/alcohol will be held.

2. Slips of paper printed with symptoms of substance abuse (lethargic, disoriented, hungry, etc) will be placed in a hat.

3. Group volunteers will randomly pick a paper slip from the hat and act out the behavior.

4. The "audience" of group members will guess the behavior and guess if alcohol or marijuana causes the symptom. As the discussion proceeds, the behaviors will be listed on the board under *marijuana* or *alcohol.*

OR the group leader can act instead of the clients.

OR this can be done to show the effects of any drug.

Idea #10

Two Face

The goal of this activity is for the students to talk about the way they *sometimes* act.

1. The group leader will share several times in which he/she acted unlike himself—his other face.

2. Next, mask molds will be distributed to the group members. The students will fill the masks with Plaster of Paris and water (the molds take approximately 30 minutes to dry).

3. When the masks dry, students will be encouraged to paint half the face like they would always like to act, and half the way they sometimes act.

4. Finally, a group discussion about the masks will be held.

Expressing Oneself: Losses, Goals

Idea #11

Sculpt a Metaphor

The goal of this activity is for the student(s) to provide clear, concrete examples of metaphors.

Activity derived from Kim Hayden, ATR-BC

1. The group facilitator should verbally introduce what constitutes a metaphor. Several examples of metaphors should be provided. For example, the facilitator/teacher can say, "The Hulk is a *house*," or "911 was a *nightmare*," or "My baby cousin is a *peanut*....What do I mean?"

2. A piece of modeling compound or clay will be given to each member of the class. The students should be allowed 15-20 minutes to sculpt and color the piece of modeling compound.

3. Each student will be allowed time to speak and explain the created metaphor and describe how it relates to him/her.

OR the students can create a metaphor from clay or modeling compound that describes a family member or friend who is important to them.

OR the students can be allowed to draw or paint as many metaphors as they can think of to describe themselves.

Idea #12

Paint an Abstract Picture That Describes Yourself

The goal for this activity is for students to express themselves via colors.

1. The personal meanings of the colors red, pink, blue, purple, yellow, white, orange, and green should be discussed with the group and written on a chalkboard. Then, the group leader will show the members of the group abstract paintings (e.g. Jackson Pollock).

2. Next, the group will have a brief discussion concerning the meanings of these abstract paintings.

3. A very brief demonstration of wet-on-wet (painting on wet paper with watercolors) will be presented.

4. Finally, the students can be allowed to experiment with sponges, watercolor paper, and brushes.

OR the group can collaborate and create an abstract watercolor painting.

OR the students can individually create abstract pictures that are representative of someone else.

Idea #13

GIVING TREE

The goal for this activity is for students to recognize the positive attributes they possess, as well as the negative attributes.

1. Before the activity, the teacher will draw a tree with no leaves on brown construction paper. *This may be laminated for re-use.*

2. Then, the students can trace around their hands on construction paper (yellow, green, and red). The cut-out hands will be the leaves of the tree. On the front of the leaf, the students will write an attribute they possess (e.g. generous, caring, giving, etc.). The students will be allowed to create as many "leaves" as they like. Next, they will paste the leaves on the tree.

3. Finally, the group will talk about the tree and the positive attributes that the participants possess.

OR students can cut pictures for magazines of people, celebrities or things they possess and glue them onto the tree.

OR the leaves or pictures can symbolize something they want to become.

AND/OR the participants can trace their hands on brown paper. These leaves can represent the negative qualities (e.g, impatient, angry, rude, etc.) that they want to get rid of. These "leaves" can be glued along the bottom of the tree to symbolize dead leaves.

Idea #14

Write a One-Page Bio

The goal for this activity is for the student to share details about him/herself.

1. The students will be encouraged to write a short biography of their lives, including struggles and dreams, on a piece of notebook paper. The group leader/teacher will check this for appropriateness and grammatical or spelling errors.

2. Then, students will rewrite their biographies on a sheet of drawing paper. The students will be encouraged to draw or decorate the paper.

Significant photos may be brought in by the students.

3. Finally, the students will pick out a mat and frame their biographies. Any pictures that the students wish to include should be glued onto the mat.

OR students can create a collage of pictures that represent their lives.

Idea #15

Mountain of Life

The goal for this activity is for students to express the HIGH times and LOW times in their lives.

1. The teacher/group leader will ask the participants to think of the *best* and *worst* incidents in their lives. The group leader will also describe one of the worst and best times in his/her life.

2. The group leader should demonstrate to the participants how to draw high and low peaks of a mountain. A word that explains the incident should be alongside the high/low peak. If time allows, colors should be added to the mountain.

3. In summation, the group/class should sit in a circle to talk about their mountain. It is hoped that this will promote discussion in the group/class, which will allow the participants to relate to and support each other.

OR the group can construct a mountain from clay that represents their "Mountain of Life."

OR students can create a plaster mold to represent their lives (students will be encouraged to use shells, feathers, sticks, etc) to symbolize their trials and successes.

Idea #16

Draw Yourself as a Cartoon Character

The goal for this activity is for students to describe character traits that are admired.

1. A brief conversation about cartoon characters should be done before the activity. The teacher/group leader can ask: "What qualities about him/her do you admire? How can you emulate those qualities? What can you do yourself to be more like the cartoon character?"

2. Then, the students can make their own cartoon character that has a special power of dealing with issues.

3. Then *any* directive (the group leader's choice) can be used to develop a short story about the cartoon character. For example, the group leader can say, "Write a story about how the character deals with bullying *OR* create a story about how the character deals with being placed in a new school."

Idea #17

Make an Album/CD Cover

The goal for this activity is for the students to describe themselves.

1. As an opener, the teacher may bring in several CDs, and the class will discuss the CD covers (front, inside, back).

2. Then, the students will be given a sheet of paper, and they will be asked to fold it in half. The students will be encouraged to design a CD cover that symbolizes them: sport photos/drawings, singing photos/drawings, animal photos/drawings, etc. Students will be allowed to use any drawing material that is available and magazine cutouts to design *the album cover that describes them.*

3. Each student will stand up and individually describe his/her album cover.

OR the students can create a CD about someone who is important to them.

OR the students can create a CD cover about someone or something that hurt them.

Idea #18

Make Your Own Record

The goal is to encourage students to talk about significant moments in their lives.

1. As an opening activity, the class will discuss the meanings of various songs on several CDs.

2. The class will be asked to think of 5-10 significant moments in their lives (e.g. a new baby was born, a birthday party, a new pet, a conflict with a parent, a conflict with a sibling, etc). Each significant moment will have a song title. For instance, the birth of a baby brother—example song title, *New Little,* or an altercation with parent—example song title, *Red Dad.*

3. After the album covers are completed, a group discussion can be held.

OR the students can make an album of the most difficult moments in their lives.

Idea #19 Follow-Up

Write One of the Songs on the Record

The goal for this activity is for the students to explain in detail a significant moment in their lives.

1. The class will discuss meanings of several favorite songs.

2. Next, the group will cut out a pre-made circle the size of a CD that fits inside their previously made CD case (Activity 17). The teacher/group leader will ask the participants to compose the lyrics to one or two songs on the record.

3. If the students chose to, they can perform the song in front of the group. Then, the group leader can ask questions based on the lyrics of the song.

Idea #20

SAD

The goal is for the group to express, explain and talk about an event or thing that made them extremely sad or hopeless. *This activity is recommended for therapists only.*

1. Students should be seated around a round table. The group leader will ask members to close their eyes and think of a situation that made them extremely sad (yesterday, last week, last month...).

2. Then, each group member will be given his/her own piece of drawing paper. Either crayons, markers, colored pencils or pastels should be placed in the middle for the participants to use. The students will be asked to draw their faces symbolizing the way they felt at that moment. Students should draw a big face surrounded by any symbols that caused that feeling. After four or five minutes, the participants will stop drawing. At this point, they will pass their drawings to the person seated on their left. Students will keep passing the drawings until their original drawing is again before them.

3. Finally, the group can have a discussion about the artwork.

OR a collaborative collage can be created by all the group members that represent a sad time in their lives.

Idea #21 Follow-Up

Happiness Is...Wait a Minute Then Pass to the Left

Follow the directions for Activity 20 on page 66, but substitute a *happy* event.

OR a collaborative collage can be created by all the group members that represent a happy time in their lives.

OR students can write the names of things they love and things that make them happy in a variety of decorative lettering styles.

Idea #22

Holding Hand

The goal for this activity is for the students to express "things" in their life that are treasured.

Activity derived from Kim Hayden, ATR-BC

1. Plaster strips will be used to create molds of the students' opened hand. Plaster tape/cloth can be purchased inexpensively at art supply stores (e.g. dickblick.com).

2. After the plaster molds are hardened (about 10 minutes), the group can decorate the hand with paint and/or use mixed media to symbolize certain things that are important to them (e.g. a heart can be painted to represent the love that is felt *or* a marble can be used to symbolize a ball, meaning sports).

3. Finally, the group will talk about their art pieces.

OR the group members can make a mold of their fists, and draw or paint the negative things about themselves that they want to terminate.

If plaster is used, when the "holding hand" is completed, it can be glued with a hot glue gun to a piece of wood; it will be a trophy or plaque that students can have forever.

Idea #23

"DREAMS"

The goal for this activity is to help students realize exactly what it is they hope to accomplish in the future.

1. The students will be asked to put their heads down and relax while the song by The Cranberries, *DREAMS* (or another appropriate song), is played 2 times.

2. Students will be asked to write a poem about what the song means to them.

3. If they are comfortable, students will be encouraged to share their poems with the group.

OR a painting or picture can be created by the students that symbolizes their dreams.

Idea #24

Success

The goal for this activity is to help the participants realize what success means to them.

1. The students will find pictures of "successful" people in magazines.

2. They will then create a story from the magazine cutouts.

OR students can draw a picture of "success."

Idea #25

Paths to Success

The goal for this activity is to help the participants realize what obstacles they have to overcome on the way to success.

1. The students will use modeling clay to sculpt representations of things they are afraid of or things that are "holding them back."

OR magazine cut-outs can be used to create a story of what students did or will overcome.

OR students can make a collage of drawings of things that were overcome.

Idea #26

Reaching the Source

The goal for this activity is for students to identify their goals and to recognize the obstacles that may stand in their way.

1. The class will be shown a pastel drawing that I created titled, *REACHING THE SOURCE.* A discussion about the meaning of the picture can be held among group members.

2. After the meaning is revealed, the students will be asked to create a 3-D assemblage representing "REACHING *THEIR* SOURCE." (Note: An assemblage is a 3-D "collage" put together from found objects.) Students will be allowed to use any art materials that are available.

3. In culmination, the group can sit in a circle and discuss their art-work.

OR the group can draw or paint a picture symbolizing *their* "source."

OR modeling compound can be used to represent their "source."

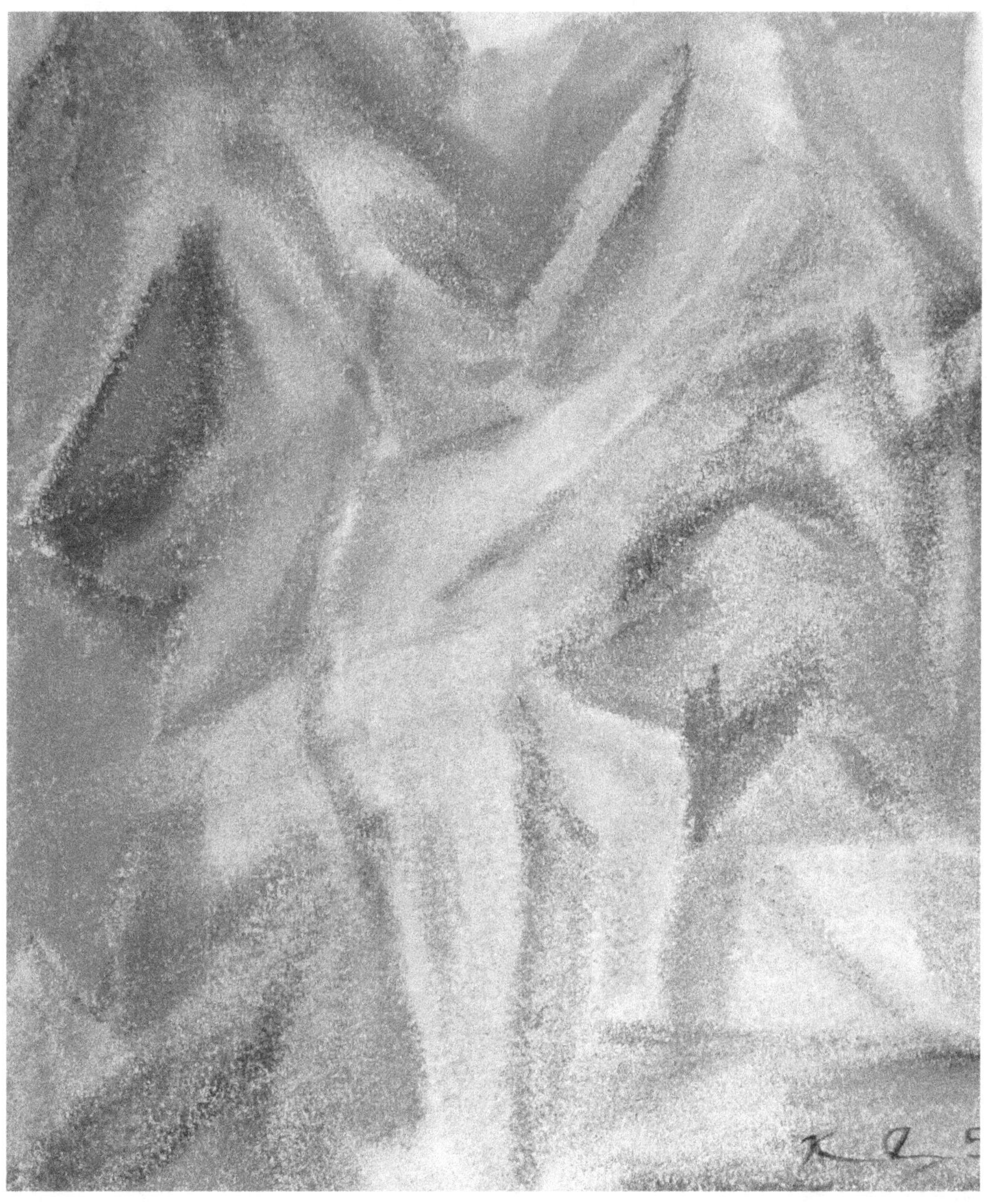

Reaching the Source, pastel drawing created in 2005.
There is a figure climbing steps to the ultimate source (goal).

NOTE: You can see *Reaching the Source* in color or buy a poster of Kevin Carey's artwork at www.avventurapress.com

Idea #27

Fairytale

The goal for this activity is for the students to create their own fairytales.

1. The group participants will write their own fairytales.
2. Then, they will assemble the fairytales into booklets.
3. Students will draw covers for their books.

Activities Concerning Family

Idea #28

Family Dynamics

The goal is to explore the levels of closeness that students feel with members of their families.

Idea from Barbara Parker-Bell, ATR-BC

1. All members of the family (mom, dad, brother, sister, grandmother, uncle, etc.) should be indicated on a large sheet of paper; a different descriptive color and shape should be assigned to each member (e.g. Mom: heart: red). A colored shape that describes the participant will also be drawn. Any paint or drawing medium can be used.

2. The students will be encouraged to draw all family members in their relation to the "closeness" that they feel to each individual.

3. Finally, a discussion about family dynamics can be held regarding the artwork created.

OR students will be given colored paper, a piece of white paper, scissors, and glue sticks. They will draw a symbol of a family member on colored paper, cut it out and paste it next to a symbol drawn on the white paper that represents themselves.

OR students can draw a metaphor that describes themselves and family members. BUT the symbols of the family members must be strategically placed in order for this art task to be successful.

OR students will be allowed to use magazines, scissors, white paper and glue sticks to find picture of persons that remind them of themselves and family members. Then the students can glue them on the white sheet of paper.

OR students will create a mask with plaster strips or papier maché to represent persons in their lives. They can then interact with the masks.

Idea #29

MAKE A FAMILY CHAIN OR BRACELET

The goal of this activity is for the student to describe family members based on colors.

Note: A jewelry kit would be ideal, but string beads and mixed media can be used.

1. The group will have a discussion a family members and jewelry.
2. The group members will be asked about what colors represent close family members.
3. Students will be allowed to work independently on their jewelry.
4. Finally, a discussion about the jewelry can be held.

OR students can make jewelry that describes them.

Idea #30

Container of Remembrance

The goal for this activity is to create an art piece to honor a person that will *always* be in one's heart.

Activity derived from Kim Hayden, ATR-BC

1. For this activity, plaster strips will be placed around one half of an inflated balloon; when the plaster strips dry, they will easily peel from the balloon, and a bowl will be created. Then, students can paint colors, symbols, or words that represent the person on the bowl.

2. The bowl can be glued onto a piece of wood or cardboard with a hot glue gun for extra support. The wood can be decorated with paint or mixed media.

3. A conversation about the bowl can be held by the students and teacher/facilitator.

OR the bowl can be representative of the student himself/herself. If this is the case, participants can be allowed to decorate it however they like.

OR the bowl can be used to hold things that are important to the student (e.g. chain, ring, ticket stub, etc.)

Idea #31

Name Acronym

The goal of this activity is to remember and honor someone students can count on in times of trouble.

1. The teacher will describe an imaginary situation in which the students find themselves in trouble. Then, the teacher will ask the class, "Who do you trust to help you?" For example, a student may say her brother Richard. The teacher will write the name *Richard* vertically on the board, then demonstrate how the name Richard can be used as an acronym: R-RELIABLE, I-INTELLIGENT, C-CARING, H-HAPPY or R-READY TO HELP, I-I KNOW HELPS PEOPLE, C-COULD CALL OTHER PEOPLE THAT MAY WANT TO HELP, etc.

2. Students will follow the same process on individual sheets of paper. A thesaurus should be available in case they get stuck on a letter.

OR students can make a name acronym about themselves.

OR a name acronym can be created about an issue (e.g. Depressed: D-DO NOT WANT TO DO ANYTHING, E-EVERYBODY IS MAD AT ME, P-PEOPLE CONSTANTLY LET ME DOWN, etc).

Idea #32

Understanding Family

The goal of this activity is for students to express qualities of family members.

1. Students will be encouraged to look through magazines to find people or things that may describe the family member.

2. Next, the students will be asked to cut them out and create a family collage.

3. Finally, a group discussion will be held about the created images.

Activities Concerning Diversity

Idea #33

Ethnic Heritage

The goal for this activity is for students to understand and appreciate different ethnic backgrounds.

A *mask may be worn by the group leader throughout the activity to teach the kids a person should NOT be judged by appearance.*

1. The group leader will write the word DIVERSITY on the board and ask students what that word means. A brief discussion of the role diversity plays in their lives can be held.

2. Students will be encouraged to browse through magazines and create a collage of diversity (e.g. people of different nationalities, foods, clothing, beverages, etc.)

3. Finally, the group will discuss the students' artwork,

OR students can make a mask that defines their heritage.

OR students can write individual poems about different heritages.

OR students can make a drawing concerning significant contributions of a certain ethnic group.

Idea #34

Contributions of Diversity in Our Country

The goal is for students to recognize contributions of diversity in the U.S.A.

1. First, pictures of famous people (e.g. Christopher Columbus) will be placed on the board. A brief lesson concerning these people's contributions will be held.

2. Then, students will be encouraged to browse through magazines to find pictures of people or things from a different nationality that made contributions to society.

3. Finally, a discussion about the participants' pictures can be held.

Idea #35

Create Your Heritage

The goal this activity is for participants to learn about different heritages.
Activity derived from Barbara Parker-Bell, ATR-BC

1. The students will be given empty boxes (e.g. shoeboxes) and they will be encouraged to decorate the box with markers, feathers, shells, etc. that symbolizes their heritage.

2. Then, the students will be given sand, sticks, feathers, magazines, etc. to create a "home" inside of the box.

3. Finally, a discussion about the ethnic features of the boxes will be held.

OR students can create masks that symbolize their unique heritages using colors, symbols and mixed media and share information about them with the class.

Idea #36

Limitations

The goal of this activity is to help the students be more aware and sympathetic of people with disabilities.

Activity derived from Mickie McGraw, ATR-BC

1. First, the group leader will tell participants about the accomplishments of "disabled people."
2. Next, the group will discuss the kind of picture they draw best.
3. Then, the students (individually) will choose a card with the name of a limitation from a box (they are pre-made). Examples include blindness, can't talk, can't use hands, etc. Students will assume the limitations through the use of blindfolds, etc.
4. Next, students will be encouraged to draw what they believe they draw best.
5. Finally, a group discussion about disabilities will be held among the group.

Miscellaneous Art Activities

Idea #37

JULY 4TH

I do this activity before the 4th of July for students to celebrate the meaning of the holiday.

1. The teacher will ask students to think of a past or upcoming event that they are really excited about (e.g. birth of a new sibling, a new bike or present, a contest that they won, etc.)

2. Then, the group will be asked to draw and/or paint the special event on the bottom portion of a large sheet of paper. Next, above the picture, mixed media will be used to create fireworks symbolizing celebration of the event. (Note: Glitter pens/glue work well for this.)

3. Finally, a discussion can be held among group members about the artwork.

Idea #38

Ideal Male/Female

The goal for this activity is for the students is for the students to explore perceptions of the "ideal qualitie"s of a male/female.

Activity derived from Barbara Parker-Bell, ATR-BC

1. First, boys and girls will be separated into 2 groups (ideally 3 or 4 group members in each). A large sheet of paper/drawing materials will be distributed to each group.

2. Next, the groups will collaboratively draw what the "quintessential male/female" looks like (The group of girls draw "perfect girl" and boys draw "perfect guy").

3. Finally, the drawings will be hung on the wall and gender stereotypes will be discussed

OR a picture of the perfect student can be created.

OR students can draw pictures individually.

OR a picture of a troublesome individual or at-risk student can be created.

Idea #39

We Are All Made of Stars

The goal of this activity is for the student to recognize his/her positive attributes.

1. First, the Moby song titled, "We are all made of stars" (one of my favorite songs) will be played two times. The students will be asked to be inspired by the song.

2. Next, students will be given pre-drawn stars photocopied onto sheets of paper They will draw pictures on the stars that are inspired by the song.

3. Then, the students will be asked to cut out the stars, write a word on each star (e. g. caring, giving, intelligent, etc) and decorate each star with crayons, pastels, markers, etc.

4. Finally, students will be encouraged to paste the stars on a separate sheet of paper and arrange them however they please.

OR a large clay star can be constructed with words or symbols that represent why the student is a "star."

Idea #40

Misunderstood

The goal for this activity is for students to express the way(s) that they are misunderstood by others.

*Art activity is recommended for a group.

1. First, the teacher will tell the class about the way(s) that I (author Kevin Carey) was misunderstood by others after my accident (e.g. I was mentally challenged, I was lazy, I was stupid, etc.).

2. Then, the teacher will ask students to draw a picture(s) of the way or ways that they are misunderstood by others.

3. Finally, participants and teacher will sit in a circle and discuss their pictures.

OR participants can create a clay sculpture that represents the way(s) that they are misunderstood.

Idea #41

Music Inspired

The goal of this activity is for students to *express* in a positive manner.

1. First, the students will be challenged to create based on a song. Personally, I choose the Beatles song titled, "Mother Nature's Son." After the song is played twice, the class will discuss the subjective meaning of the song.

2. Then, for the next session, students will be asked to create a story based on the song's lyrics (this will be done at home).

3. During the next session, a large sheet of paper will be folded in half to be a book cover. The students will be encouraged to give their stories a title and decorate the book covers.

4. Students will continue to work on their stories in future sessions. Suggestions and revisions will be made by the teacher or therapist.

OR A clay piece that is inspired by the song can be created.

Idea #42

The Head

The goal for this activity is to help students focus on important issues.

1. The group leader will talk to the kids about significant occurrences in their lives.

2. Then, a large sheet of drawing paper will be given to each student. They will draw a large profile of a head (The group leader will demonstrate on his or her own sheet.)

3. Next, the group leader will explain how either dwelling on or suppressing issues may harm personal well-being. The group leader will describe some of the hurtful and good things that happened in his or her life. Then, the group leader will ask the students where words or symbols that describe the events should be placed on the drawing of his/her head.

4. Finally, students will work independently with various drawing materials to create their heads.

Idea #43

Emotions Mask

The goal of this activity is to artistically and verbally explain the students' "other face."

1. The teacher will describe several things that happened in his or her life that evoked "another face." Examples include rude people that the teacher came across, loss of loved ones, etc). Then, the teacher will ask the students to create a mask of their "other" face.

2. First a mask mold of plaster will be made (Plastic molds in the form of faces can be found in art supply catalogs).

3. When it dries, the plaster will be popped from the mold. Students will be allowed to paint and/or add mixed media to the face.

Idea #44

Admiration

The goal of this activity is for the students to express qualities that they admire about a person.

1. First sheets of paper, scissors and glue sticks will be distributed to students.
2. Students will be encouraged to browse through pile of magazines to find pictures of people that they admire and cut them out.
3. Next, students will create a collage of admiration with the pictures.
4. Finally, a discussion about the artwork will be held by the group.

Idea #45

T-shirt of Honor

The goal of this activity is for the students to identify someone or something that will always be respected.

1. First, the group leader will identify a person and a place that are respected.

2. Next, t-shirts and fabric markers will be distributed to students. Students will be encouraged to create a shirt depicting someone that is respected.

3. Finally, a group discussion about the t-shirts will be held.

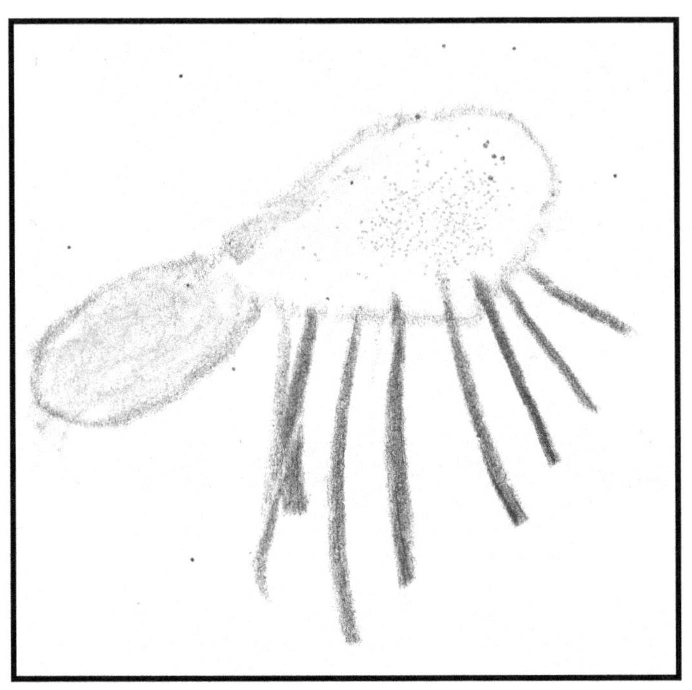

Part V

Resources

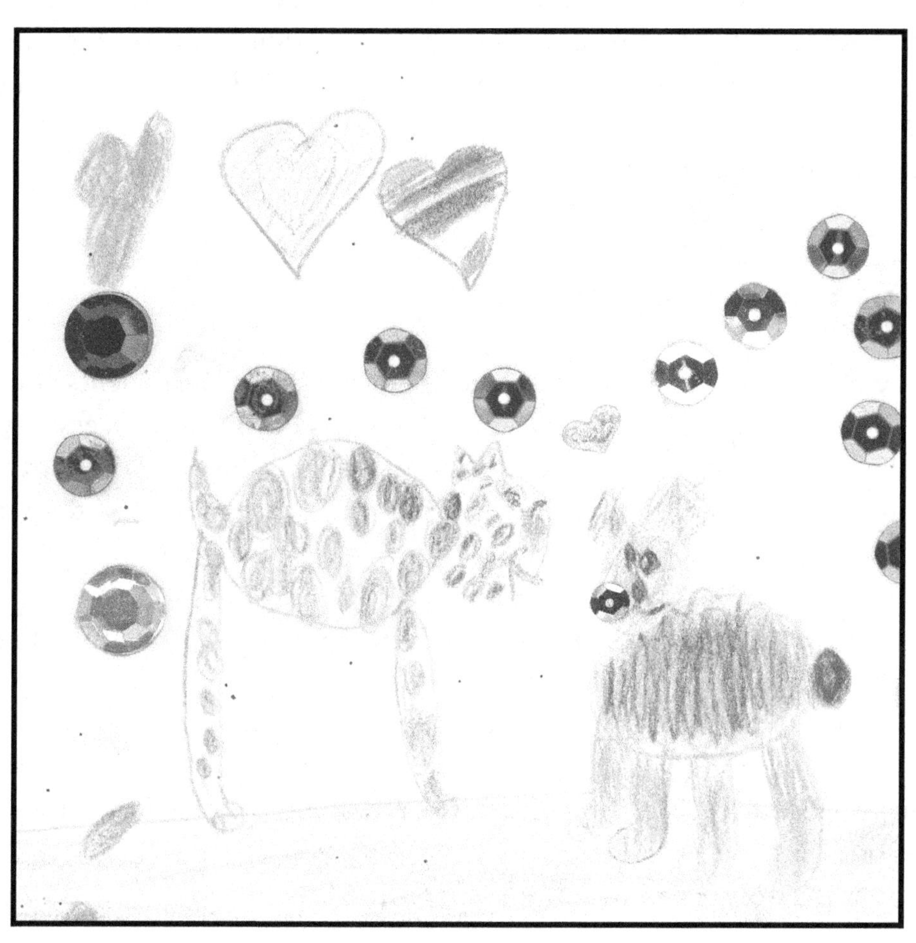

Art Therapy in Schools

A licensed art therapist brings unique benefits to a school district's therapeutic support staff. If you would like to encourage your local district to engage an art therapist, you may wish to refer the administrstion to the **American Art Therapy Association** Website. You can find a local art therapist in their Art Therapist Locator database and read some interesting articles by clicking on Art Therapy in the News.
`http://www.arttherapy.org`

Art Therapy and Children

The Websites, books and articles listed below describe the benefits and techniques of art therapy with children. Art therapy has been used successfully with children who are survivors of natural disasters, sexual abuse and other traumas, as well as with bereaved children and children with behavioral and attention disorders.

The Art Connection is an exemplary program for at-risk students in the Chicago Public School System.
`http://www.arttherapyconnection.org`

Connect For Kids is a children's advocacy group. Its arts page offers news updates on art's benefits for children.
`http://www.connectforkids.org/about`

Medical art therapy can help children who are facing health issues. Here is a book chapter excerpt:
`http://tracyskids.org/pdf/Malchiodi-Ch16.pdf`

Children with **learning disabilities** can benefit from art therapy. Here is an overview:
`http://www.ldonline.org/article/5817`

The **National Art Education Association** Website includes several publications describing the educational benefits of art, including advocacy resources.
`http://www.naea-reston.org`

Here is a *New York Tiimes* article about art therapy with children who are survivors of **Hurricane Katrina**.
`http://www.nytimes.com/2007/09/17/arts/design/17ther.html`

Books

You can find these books on Amazon.com and other online retailers as well as order them from your favorite bookstore. Check your local library and its interlibrary loan program, too.

Art Therapy in Schools: Effective Integration of Art Therapists in Schools by Dafna Moriya. Published by D. Moriya, 2000. 78 pages. ISBN: 978-0398068684

Art Therapy Activities: A Practical Guide for Teachers, Therapists and Parents by Pamela J. Stack. Published by Charles C. Thomas, 2006. 134 pages. ISBN: 978-0398076719

Understanding Children's Drawings by Cathy Malchiodi. Published by Guilford, 1998. 252 pages. ISBN: 978-1572303720

Transcending: An Artist's Journey Back From Traumatic Brain Injury by Kevin D. Carey. Published by Avventura Press, 2006. 116 pages. ISBN: 978-0976155300

Kevin's first book tells the powerful story of his tragic automobile accident and how his love of art and the support of his family and friends led him to his new life as an artist and therapist. Eight pages of color photos.

Transcending can be ordered from www.avventurapress.com. Bulk pricing of *Transcending* and *Draw-Bridges* is available from Avventura Press. Inquire about fund-raising opportunities.

Kevin Carey is available for presentations to school and community groups. Contact lee@avventurapress.com for more information.

Kevin's artwork is available for sale at www.yessy.com.

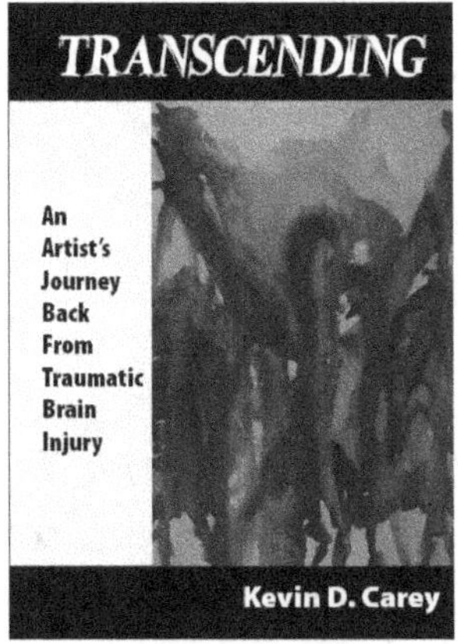

Articles

The reference librarian at your library can help you find these articles.

Art Therapy for Children: How It Leads to Change by Diane Waller
Source: Clinical Child Psychology and Psychiatry, Vol 11(2), Apr. 2006. pp. 271-282.

The Art of Healing by Marianne Szegedy-Maszak
Source: U.S. News & World Report: 9/11/2002 Special Issue, Vol. 133, p36.

Chaos to Calm by Diana Hinds
Source: Times Educational Supplement: 11/30/2007 Issue 4765, special section p. 50-51.

Healing Through Art Therapy in Disaster Settings by S. Haroon Ahmed and Naim Siddiqi
Source: Lancet: Dec. 2006 Supplement, Vol. 368, p. 28-29.

Arts, Education and Society: The Role of the Arts in Promoting the Emotional Wellbeing and Social Inclusion of Young People
by Vassiliki Karkou and Judy Glasman
Source: Support for Learning: May 2004, Vol. 19 Issue 2, p/ 57-65.

Brush on Paint, Swirl in Some Glitter, And Suddenly Everything Looks Better
by Alice Reid
Source: Washington Post: 12/31/2007, p. B03

The Power of A.R.T. by Maria A. Tortoreto
Source: The Exceptional Parent v. 34 no. 7 (July 2004) p. 52-3.

www.ingramcontent.com/pod-product-compliance
Lightning Source LLC
LaVergne TN
LVHW061225100826
845148LV00004B/860

* 9 7 8 0 9 7 6 1 5 5 3 2 4 *